Jason Rebello was born in Mumbai, India, and went to sea at the early age of seventeen. He spent many years sailing across the world on modern ocean liners, eventually rising to the rank of a ship's Captain. His sea career was interspaced with a healthy dose of backpacking and intrepid travels and as a result he was firmly hooked on a life of adventure and uncommon living. His travel blog www.theevolvingbackpacker.com was born out of his passion for travel. He has also written several self-help books in the 'Migrant Ninja' series.

Jason, with his wife and two children, is now settled in Australia.

RED EARTH DIARIES

JASON REBELLO

For one year from the date it is first published, five percent of all profits from the sale of this book will be donated to the Red Cross towards bushfire crisis management (www.redcross.org.au) and an additional five percent will be donated to aged care in India through Help Age India (www.helpageindia.org).

First published by Evolving Wordsmith in 2021
ISBN 978-0-9945674-5-1 (Print - Rest of world)
ISBN 978-0-9945674-7-5 (Print - Indian subcontinent)
ISBN 978-0-9945674-6-8 (Digital)

All rights reserved. Without limiting the rights under copyright below, no part of this publication shall be reproduced, stored in or introduced into a retrieval system, or transmitted in any form or by any means (electronic, mechanical, photocopying, recording or otherwise), without the prior permission of both the copyright holder and the publisher.

The moral right of the author has been asserted.
Copyright © Evolving Wordsmith 2020
Edited by Rod Morrison
Some names have been changed to protect the identity of certain persons.

WARNING: Aboriginal and Torres Strait Islander readers are warned that this book may contain references to and words of deceased persons.

Follow the adventures:
www.theevolvingbackpacker.com
www.evolvingwordsmith.com
An Evolving Wordsmith Product.
For more information email: info@evolvingwordsmith.com

*To my dad, Thomas, who taught me to live simply,
feel deeply and tread fearlessly.*

To India, for setting me off on my backpacking adventures.

*To Australia, for providing me with a blank canvas
and the chance for a fresh start.*

*To Ambika, my travel partner, without whom this journey
would never have unfolded.*

Table Of Contents

PREFACE: Dreamtime ... xi
CHAPTER 1: The Master Plan ... 1
CHAPTER 2: Lift Off ... 7
CHAPTER 3: Two Backpacks and a Business Suit ... 13
CHAPTER 4: A River Runs Through It ... 18
CHAPTER 5: Of Strange Beasts and Distant Lands ... 23
CHAPTER 6: Heads we go North! ... 31
CHAPTER 7: Sea Creatures ... 38
CHAPTER 8: Romancing the Railways ... 49
CHAPTER 9: Heart of the Reef ... 55
CHAPTER 10: Flight of Fancy ... 62
CHAPTER 11: Ancient Land and Old Culture ... 69
CHAPTER 12: Inside a Picture Postcard ... 78
CHAPTER 13: Where the Rainforest meets the Reef ... 86
CHAPTER 14: Shipwrecked ... 96
CHAPTER 15: Daal, Roti and War Stories ... 104
CHAPTER 16: Adieu to Queensland ... 113
CHAPTER 17: The Gold Rush ... 120
CHAPTER 18: The Grand Dame ... 127
CHAPTER 19: Twelve Apostles ... 137
CHAPTER 20: The Valley of Fine Wines ... 145
CHAPTER 21: Seat of Power ... 150

CHAPTER 22: Dark Caves and New Discoveries ... 158
CHAPTER 23: Into the Blue ... 164
CHAPTER 24: Emerald City ... 168
CHAPTER 25: Showers of Blessings ... 177
EPILOGUE: Land of the Red Dog ... 186
BIBLIOGRAPHY ... 191
ACKNOWLEDGEMENTS ... 196

PREFACE
Dreamtime

Maybe it won't work out. But maybe seeing if it does will be the best adventure ever – Unknown

Desire is a strange and powerful thing. So too is imagination. Sometimes in life, when they conspire, it can lead to unimaginable and extraordinary outcomes and we can realise our wildest dreams. Seeds are sown in the far corners of the mind – purely random aspirations on purely random days. Time passes by and some of these seeds are discarded. Some fail to germinate due to unfavourable conditions. Some struggle to grow and eventually die a slow death. But every so often, the universe aligns itself to create perfect conditions and one such seed of an idea is able to germinate – to see the light of day, to flourish and to bear fruit.

This story is about one such dream which, until a few years ago, seemed outlandish and fanciful – even to me – a dream of migrating to Australia, and of living a life of unlimited adventure.

I vividly remember the day I first imagined a life 'Down Under'. The year was 1994, and I was a young marine cadet aboard an ocean-going ship called the *Darya Chand*, a 35,000-tonne general cargo vessel. Being employed in a 'tramping trade', the *Darya Chand* sailed around the world carrying grain, steel products, coal and fertiliser, among other goods. In my first six months aboard, I visited many exotic and far-flung ports – Japan, the USA, Thailand and Singapore, to name just a few.

I had turned seventeen a few months before setting sail; being underage, my mother had to accompany me to the Shipping Master's office to sign the shipping indenture on my behalf. I was considered a juvenile – a soft lump of clay ready to be moulded by the hands of destiny and equally eager to soak up all experiences along the way. A sea career meant a lifetime of travel and freedom – freedom from university studies, from mundanity, from everyday worries. From an early age I had a penchant for adventure and had always harboured a desire for exploring faraway places and unconventional paths. Life at sea would give me an opportunity to do all this and more.

The *Darya Chand* had just docked in Brisbane, Queensland's capital, and I was due some shore leave. I got dressed in my Sunday best, scrubbed and groomed like a choir boy for high mass, eager to explore the sights of a new country. The sky was a faultless blue, and the eucalypts that lined the old port road leading to the seafarer's club infused the air with crispness. I planned to grab a bite to eat at the McDonald's in town, after which I'd go shopping for some souvenirs. As I approached the town centre, I remember seeing this young guy, clearly a local, with dishevelled blond hair and tattooed arms, dressed casually in a pair of boardshorts and a loose-fitting singlet. He was barefoot and seemingly without a care in the world – and no one seemed to find it the slightest bit unusual.

For some inexplicable reason, my teenage brain decided to tag this inconsequential piece of data, equate it with 'freedom, travel and uncommon living' and preserve it for a later date.

Time went by. My career progressed and I rose up the ranks, ultimately sailing as a captain on giant ocean liners. I circumnavigated the globe, crossed the international dateline and traversed the equator umpteen times. I visited countless ports, each with a unique appeal. However, every now and again, the thought of that random Australian man walking barefoot in Brisbane kept popping up. Without any conscious effort, this thought gradually became a desire, and I slowly began imagining how it would be to migrate to Australia and settle down.

Then again, the vagabond in me held similar thoughts of migrating to most of the other countries I'd visited – USA, Mexico, France, Germany, Japan and even China, although not with the same level of seriousness. Of course, these were just random thoughts. I was enjoying a comfortable life in India. Over the years, I had turned into a hardened sailor and an intrepid backpacker. While not at sea, I preferred travelling to remote destinations over city living; the unfamiliarity of the open road over the constant company of society. My life was sorted.

And then one day Cupid struck like a bolt of lightning.

My mother, concerned I was going to die a lonely death in some far-flung corner of the world, would wring her hands in despair. Every time I came home for holidays, with the stereotypical melodrama of an Indian mother, she'd cajole and convince me into meeting a 'suitable bride'. This kind of 'arranged marriage' system – although an age-old Indian tradition, irrespective of religion or culture – is actually quite similar to modern online dating and matchmaking sites. In more recent times, the role of a parent has been limited to checking the family background – ensuring there's no cultural or social mismatch – and making the initial introductions.

My modus operandi in these situations was simple. I would go on the first date (which more often than not turned out to be the last) only to talk myself and my prospective bride out of the proposal. I would explain that I had a rare but acute case of 'itchy feet' and a worsening case of 'explorer syndrome'. These conditions, I would argue, prevented me from lying still in the comforts of home for an extended period of time. Understandably, most of the girls wasted no time finishing their coffees and making a dash for the nearest exit. To be fair, they thought they were meeting someone intending to settle down, not gallivant around the world.

Ambika, on the other hand, turned out to be a very different kettle of fish.

We first met towards the end of 2012. On our first coffee 'date' I rattled off my well-practised speech about why I preferred to be single. 'Nothing personal,' I said, 'it's just that I don't see myself ever starting a family or staying in one place for the rest of my life. You seem like a lovely girl, and I'm sure you'll meet the right person who'll bring you a lot of happiness, but that person just ain't me.'

So firm was my conviction that I never really expected someone to ever challenge it. Ambika was the first and only person who did. She gazed at me in silence for a minute, slowly sipping her coffee and regarding me with her mesmerising amber eyes. Then she asked, 'Did it ever occur to you that you could have a life partner *and* still travel to your heart's content? Why would anyone ask you to give up something that you're so passionate about, especially if that person was hoping to be your life partner?'

It was my turn to be rattled and, for the first time ever, I began contemplating a travel partner. That first date led to a series of catch-ups and with every meeting, my defences slowly crumbled. It wasn't long before I got down on one knee and proposed. From that moment, I knew that my life had irrevocably changed. She said yes, by the way.

It turned out Ambika loved exploring as much as I did, having done a fair bit of it in India as a child with her family. Later, she had also travelled overseas on multiple occasions in her role as a sales manager. I was soon to discover that she had an equally adventurous streak.

We were in the starry-eyed phase of our courtship where everything around us seemed picture-perfect – the skies were bluer than they had ever been, the birds chirped in the most melodious tones, the flowers were in full bloom. The world was ours for the taking. All we had to do was paint the most colourful picture on the blank canvas of our life together. In between working out the wedding arrangements and gazing into the crystal ball, we began fantasising about all the exciting voyages we would embark upon once we were married. Ambika eventually proved to be the catalyst for realising my life-long dream of migrating to Australia.

Sailors are never short of imagination – where do you think all the 'mermaid' and 'treasure island' stories come from? – but again, Ambika, who turned out to be a feisty sparring partner, was not to be outdone. One evening while walking along the foreshore of the Arabian Sea in Bandra, a glitzy suburb of Mumbai, oblivious to the crowds that swarmed around us on the promenade, I casually broached the topic of moving overseas permanently, hoping not to alarm her with my outlandish proposition. At that time, we were settled, at the peak of our careers, had our families close by and were living a comfortable life. We had no real reason to migrate.

'Let's set sail to a land far, far away,' I said.

'Sure,' Ambika replied, wondering where this conversation was leading.

'How about moving to a country where the sun shines all through the year?'

'Hmm … sounds great. Where do you think that is?'

'How about Australia?' I asked in a flat monotone that belied my nervousness. 'It's a beautiful country, the people seem lovely, and it could be a wonderful place to start a family.'

Ambika gazed silently out towards the distant horizon for a few minutes which seemed like an eternity to me. Then she turned and said in a steadfast voice, 'Yes, I think we should give it a go.'

And just like that, that tiny seed of desire from two decades earlier finally emerged, triumphant and glorious.

The next few months flew by in a flurry of activity as we prepared for the marriage celebrations – and visa applications. It was sometime during this phase that I made the most daring proposition to Ambika yet.

'Will you shed all reservations, not worry about the future and backpack with me across Australia instead of settling down as soon as we get there? Why don't we leave all our worries – of getting a job, buying a house, having babies – until later?' I knew that this was a wild stab in the dark. I was already uprooting Ambika from her family, her friends, her job and her country. I was now asking her to postpone setting up a home for the sake of an extended vacation in a foreign land. Surely, the answer would be a resounding 'no'.

She looked deep into my eyes and in a tone that belied her excitement, said, 'Hell yes! I reckon it'll be quite an adventure!'

This then is our story. Of how two newlywed, first-time migrants threw caution to the wind and embraced a new country. It's a story of our journey in a strange and foreign land – jobless, with no prospective employment and without a permanent roof over our heads. We had no real action plan except to follow the road of discovery for as long as we could sustain ourselves. To make matters more challenging, we were earning in Indian rupees and spending in Australian dollars. But being smart was not part of our strategy. We had the rest of our lives for that. Apart from satiating our appetite for adventure, backpacking across Australia would help us learn more about the country and its people first-hand. What a frightfully exciting prospect.

(Our travel story is intertwined with snippets of Australian history as seen through the eyes of newly arrived migrants, and includes interlude chapters - about the peculiarities that define this land, the pioneers and adventurers that forged its identity, and the watershed events that shaped the nation.)

This book represents the fruition of all my impossible fantasies and the realisation of my deepest desires – of meeting the girl of my dreams, of migrating to Australia, of living a life of unlimited adventure, of writing and publishing a book and of starting a beautiful family in a land far far away. Hold onto your dreams, I tell you. You never know which one of them may come true!

CHAPTER 1
The Master Plan

Two roads diverged in a wood, and I took the one less travelled, and that has made all the difference – Robert Frost

4 March 2014 – Great Belt Bridge, Denmark.
'Rudder port ten, engines slow ahead,' I ordered as my ship the *Viona*, a 3500-TEU (twenty-foot equivalent) container vessel, passed Samso, the tiny Danish island in the Kattegat. The helmsman smartly executed my command, rounding the bend with great finesse while Ilsa, my First Officer, a young and energetic German woman, verified our position by laying bearings from the prominent landmarks on the coastline.

One of the few entry points to the Baltic Sea, the Kattegat passage is a busy and treacherous waterway. The entire region is a maze of fractured islands, shallow waters and tricky currents which test the skills of all mariners. A vital sea route, the strait is used by large container ships, oil tankers and cruise ships alike and provides a crucial link between the Baltic countries and Europe and the rest of the world. Navigating is difficult even in calm weather and clear visibility is a rare occurrence in these higher latitudes. During severe winters, it's not uncommon for sections of the Baltic Sea to freeze, with ice occasionally drifting out of the straits, carried by the surface currents.

The ship I was commandeering was on a back-and-forth 'pendulum' run, stopping at the ports of St Petersburg (Russia), Kotka (Finland), Gdańsk (Poland), Aarhus (Denmark) and Klaipėda (Lithuania) in the Baltic Sea, and Bremerhaven (Germany) and Rotterdam (Netherlands) in the North Sea. On this particular trip, the weather gods were in a benevolent mood and we were transiting under a faultless blue sky in one of the most picturesque regions of the world. The strait got narrower as we sailed closer to Zealand (Sjælland), the largest of the off-lying Danish islands. Up ahead, as we zigzagged through the labyrinth of islands, the tall and majestic Great Belt Bridge sprang into view. The pylons lift the suspension bridge some sixty-five metres above sea level allowing it to accommodate the largest of the ocean cruise liners that frequently pass under its dominating expanse.

As the *Viona* glided beneath the towering bridge, the bow waves created lazy ripples and twirling eddies in an otherwise calm sea. The placid waters and the stunning scenery made the perfect backdrop for reminiscing, and I found myself mulling over the frantic activity of the last few months. Meeting Ambika, although premeditated in a way by our well-meaning parents, had changed my life. Not only had I fallen in love and gotten married within a few months of having met Ambika, but I had also filed our immigration papers and we were potentially moving to Australia by the end of the year. Everything now hinged on the Australian Immigration Department's decision. The wait time was expected to be a couple of months.

As much as I loved the seafaring life, I was about to bid adieu to my career and step ashore for good. If things went to plan, and we were granted our migration papers, this tenure aboard the *Viona* would mark the final chapter of my two decades at sea. I could not have chosen a sturdier ship, a better crew or a more exciting voyage.

The cold winter draught was sharp. We were due to encounter ice as the ship headed into the frigid waters of the Baltic Sea en route to St Petersburg, our first port of call. We had cleared the trickiest section of the Great Belt transit, rounding the tiny island of Fehmarn – the place where Jimi Hendrix gave his last performance in 1970 – and I handed over the control of the vessel to my First Officer. Just then, my phone beeped excitedly. It was Ambika. She had cryptically messaged, 'Call when possible. Something is up'.

I ducked out onto the bridge wing and called her straight away, suppressing my eagerness and withholding my worst fears. Ambika was on her lunch break and the incessant sounds of the city made it hard for me to hear her clearly. I initially mistook her excitement for worry when she blurted something about our visa. 'Honey, our visa papers have ...' but the rest of the message got garbled as we moved out of coverage. I paced nervously up and down the bridge wing, waiting to get within signal range again. After about fifteen minutes and two quick shots of espresso, I was able to reconnect with Ambika, and this time she got the message across loud and clear. 'Honey, our migration papers have come through! We're going Down Under!' I was barely able to contain my excitement, but stopped short of breaking into a victory dance on the bridge. Not a good look for a ship's captain.

Stage one of our migration – obtaining our permanent resident visas – was now complete. This was the most crucial step, knowing how stringent Australian immigration laws were, but it was easy compared to the next stage – actually moving to a foreign country for good. Would we be successful and be able to live a comfortable life in Australia? Or would we have to return to India? Time would tell. One thing was sure: I would take this opportunity and make it count.

More concerned with our backpacking trip, I paid little heed to the faint voice of caution which counselled me to think about what came after that. I bought a copy of the *Lonely Planet Guide* to Australia (a colossal volume that would put an encyclopedia to shame) and began mapping out an itinerary. The deciding factor for the length of the trip was financial and we set ourselves a budget of $10,000 or sixty days of travel time. As soon as we hit either of these milestones, we'd pull the plug and focus on the next stage of our journey – settling down and getting a job. We may have been bold, but we were definitely not brash. We set ourselves a target of six months to find employment. Hopefully, one of us would be successful by then, and we could start to build our nest, one Australian dollar at a time.

The issue that many travellers (and we were no different) face when visiting Australia is that they picture it as just another country, much like India or Germany or even the USA. However, Australia is most certainly not just another country but rather a vast continent; an immense landmass that spans three time zones. Until the eighteenth century, the existence of this mega-landmass was a fancy hypothesis, albeit with some merit: 'Surely there has to be a giant continent somewhere in the southern hemisphere to balance all the landmasses in the northern hemisphere?'

In terms of land size, Australia is nearly twenty-two times bigger than Germany and roughly twice the size of India. It soon became apparent that in mapping out our itinerary, we were metaphorically scraping too little butter on too much bread.

We initially thought we could cover the entire east coast, starting from Darwin in the 'top end' (as Australians like to call the Northern Territory), working our way leisurely south, covering most of Queensland, before moving onto New South Wales and Victoria before proceeding inland to Uluru. We also wanted to visit Perth on the west coast. This was too ambitious. We soon learnt Perth and Darwin are closer to Asia than cities on the eastern seaboard! Flying the 3600 kilometres from Brisbane to Perth would take around five hours.

Apart from the size, the other factor we had to consider was the cost. Although flying was the cheapest option, it was not the best way to truly get to know Australia. You got to see more on a bus, but routes were limited to major networks and backtracking would prove expensive. Trains were expensive; while renting a car, especially for two people, was the most flexible. However, driving was not without its own risks and expense, chiefly fatigue and parking fees and tolls in capital cities.

The Master Plan

We didn't just want to see the sights, we wanted to feel the heartbeat of the nation, understand the ethos of the land, buy into the culture of this diverse and multicultural society and interact with real Aussies. At the forefront of all our considerations was the fact that we wanted to settle down with an unbiased and unprejudiced view of the people. This would only be possible if we made an effort to learn the culture first-hand.

At the end of our planning phase, we drew the following conclusions:

1. Travel was expensive
2. Distances were vast
3. The land and the seas were fraught with wild and exotic creatures
4. The country could be divided into three broad categories – beaches, forests and the outback.

But we still had no clue where to start and where to finish.

We finally ended up doing what any self-respecting backpacker would do: we pinned a large map of Australia on the wall, did a bit of a thumb suck and without any further deliberation picked a starting point – Brisbane. It seemed like a logical place. It was almost at the centre of the eastern coastline and was well connected. The direction of our travel and all subsequent destinations would eventuate as a natural progression once we commenced our tour of the country … or so we hoped!

Our final itinerary looked like this: heading north from Brisbane, we visited the Sunshine Coast, the Whitsundays, Mackay, Townsville, Cairns, Port Douglas and Cape Tribulation. We then turned south, flying to Melbourne and spending some time there, before heading to the Great Ocean Road, Port Campbell, the Yarra Valley, Canberra and the Blue Mountains. We ended our trip in Australia's most iconic city – Sydney. We used a mix of transport: budget airlines, interstate buses, trains, rental cars … even hitchhiking on one occasion!

As our journey unfolded, we learnt more and more about Australia every day. Our fears and apprehensions were replaced with wonder and amazement at how weirdly peculiar and utterly beautiful this land and its people are. We were left poorer in the pocket but richer in our experience. In the end, we ran out of money before we ran of time, but it was an amazing journey of discovery.

CHAPTER 2
Lift Off

Start by doing what's necessary; then do what's possible, and suddenly you are doing the impossible – St Francis of Assisi

'Boarding pass and passport,' the bored immigration officer said, stifling a yawn as we approached his desk at Mumbai international airport. We obediently handed over the paperwork, hoping this would be over quickly. The immigration officer scanned the documents repeatedly as if looking for a reason to hold us back. 'What's your final destination and purpose of travel?' he asked.

'We're migrating to Australia,' we chimed in, smiling broadly as if expecting a pat on the back. We then proudly flashed our Australian visa grant notices. The officer did not seem impressed and went back to inspecting our documents, turning them upside down a couple of times as if trying to decipher a secret code. With an air of authority, and almost reluctantly it would seem, he embossed the exit stamp on our passports and dismissed us with a wave of his hand, instantly losing interest as he summoned the next passengers in the queue.

As we left the checkpoint, it seemed as though we were passing over some invisible Indian border. We gave our birth country one longing look back before hopping on the escalator and proceeding to the departure gate.

We were flying to Brisbane via Kuala Lumpur, a journey of around fifteen hours, including the brief transit stop. Australia was a long way from anywhere yet modern aviation had made travel so convenient and affordable that no one thought of it as difficult or hazardous anymore. Today's travel woes centred around overcoming jet lag or figuring out your duty-free limits. I tried to imagine life in the eighteenth century when the First Fleet made the long and arduous sea voyage from Great Britain. Air travel was yet to be invented, steam-powered ships were still decades away and the sailing vessels that arrived in 1788 took over a hundred days to reach Sydney.

The advent of aviation made Australia more accessible, however flying long distance in the mid-1900s was not much fun. I'm glad I wasn't born back then. Imagine the options – sail for weeks on end through uncharted waters or take your chance flying in an aeroplane. The first Qantas service from Brisbane to London on 13 April 1935 took twelve long, eventful days to make the 12,753-mile journey. (Eventually, the 'kangaroo route' between Australia and the UK became so famous that the leaping marsupial was chosen as the airline's logo.) Until the introduction of jets in the late 1950s, most commercial planes were propeller-driven, unpressurized, and had a maximum cruising altitude of 12,000 feet. Flying in bad weather was not a pleasant experience, jaw-shuddering turbulence was commonplace and there were frequent delays. The safety record of the aviation industry during that era was atrocious with nearly a dozen crashes *every year* in the late 1940s.

Some travellers have all the luck when flying – free upgrades, premium seats and complimentary lounge access. Ambika and I, on the other hand, represent the other half of the commuters – our fate comprises back row seats, stacked overhead compartments, wobbly tray tables and quirky fellow passengers.

For the first leg of our journey to Kuala Lumpur, my neighbour was an elderly British lady named Elise. Elise was travelling with her husband

and the way she frequently cast furtive glances up the aisles, it appeared that she may have lost him somewhere along the way – I later realised that he was sitting a few rows in front of us. Elise's chief concern, apart from educating us on the dangers lurking in Australia, was not to lose her husband again and she took every opportunity to check on his wellbeing. Every time she came back to her seat she felt obliged to report to me that he was doing marvellously. I would meekly smile as if to say, 'Well, that's a relief, isn't it? I shall await your next hourly report then.'

We barely noticed taking off at Mumbai, turning west over the Arabian Sea as the plane steadily gained altitude, before banking eastwards. The city lights twinkled like distant stars below, the 'Queen's Necklace' off Marine Drive in South Mumbai so breathtakingly beautiful, silently fading away as the bank of stubby cumulus clouds gradually obscured the view. It was like the slow and deliberate lowering of the velvet curtains at the end of a grand musical. Hard not to feel sad as the invisible cord that tied us to India was finally severed in one decisive stroke.

It transpired that Elise and her husband Jack were on a three-month holiday across Asia. After having spent a fortnight in India (which they 'loved'), they were now visiting Malaysia, Singapore and Vietnam. They had done the well-trodden traveller circuit called the 'Golden Triangle' in the north of India, covering Delhi, Agra and Jaipur. They had also spent some time in the south-western state of Kerala, delving into traditional ayurvedic treatments. Obviously well-travelled, Elise and Jack had been retired for a few years now and were on a mission to explore the world in the golden phase of their lives. They'd never been to Australia though and were excited – but apprehensive.

'Don't go swimming,' Elise said in a hushed tone, 'the waters are *infested* with sharks and crocodiles. I've heard that the crocodiles prey on unwary tourists even in the lakes and estuaries.' She shuddered involuntarily. 'Why, only recently I read an article about a British couple who went snorkelling in the Great Barrier Reef and the man was attacked by a great white shark!'

'That's probably not correct,' I said. 'Great whites aren't usually seen in the Great Barrier Reef area. You'd have a better chance of spotting them in New South Wales or Western Australia. Tiger sharks are probably the most fearsome of the lot around the reef, but most of these creatures tend to keep to themselves.' I glanced at Ambika as I said this and gave her a reassuring nod. 'Statistically speaking, you have a higher chance of a car crash or of being hit by a bus than getting bitten by a shark.'

'Oh yes,' Elise said, latching onto my mention of car crashes, 'you need to be careful there, too. Those iconic bouncing kangaroos can be quite a nuisance, I'm told. Take care when driving as they're a real hazard on the highways. You wouldn't be wanting to have one of them come bounding on the motorway when you're doing 110 kilometres per hour!' She barely paused for breath. 'And be *particularly* careful when travelling *anywhere* in the outback. I've read numerous stories where tourists have gone missing ... *never* to be found.' By this point, she was leaning across me, her ample bosom resting unapologetically on my arm as she directed her advice to Ambika. She seemed to be suggesting that men did not perceive threats gravely and it was the women folk who were charged with the role of keeping the family safe. 'I've seen a documentary on *National Geographic* that said that Australia has some of the most venomous snakes and spiders lurking in the bushes. Be sure to stay on the main tracks and don't go wandering around.'

'The country also has cute koalas and furry wombats,' I said, hoping to steer the conversation towards safer territory and allay Ambika's fears. Luckily for me, the meal and the wine got the better of Elise and she was soon snoring away, most probably dreaming about giant crocodiles and slithering snakes.

Australia does have some of the planet's most dangerous animals, and a large part of the country faces extreme weather conditions, but it's also a land of stunning landscapes and unparalleled natural beauty. It has one of the world's longest coastlines, hundreds of picturesque beaches, lush tropical rainforests and world-class wineries and agricultural regions. The country is a prime tourist destination, receiving over seven million visitors a year. Popular destinations include the coastal cities of Sydney, Brisbane and Melbourne, as well as other high-profile places such as regional Queensland, the Gold Coast, the Great Barrier Reef, Uluru and the Tasmanian wilderness.

Part of the success of Australia's tourism industry can be credited to the government's efforts to package the remote region to the outside world. Up until the 1980s, Australia was an enigma, a faraway and inaccessible land full of quaint and exotic animals – hopping kangaroos, cuddly koalas, chubby wombats and the weirdly wonderful platypus. That the country was also inhabited by some of the most forward-thinking and easy-going people had escaped many. Then in January 1984, during a National Football League game in Los Angeles, an innocuous ad campaign was launched promoting Australia as an offbeat tourist destination. The face of the campaign was one Paul Hogan, a lean, witty and down-right genuine bloke who invited the world to 'come and say g'day', cheekily adding the line, 'I'll slip an extra shrimp on the barbie for you.' With his characteristic Australian twang and his carefree manner, Hogan clicked with the American psyche.

Two years later, in 1986, Hogan appeared again in front of the American audience, this time in a low-budget film called *Crocodile Dundee*. Costing just over $7 million to make, the film went on to become a huge success, raking in over $300 million at the box office and catapulting Hogan to international stardom. It also brought the magic of Australia – and the unique Australian ethos – into millions of homes around the world.

The floodgates were finally open. Suddenly, the world stood up and took notice of Australia – its people, its ancient rainforests, the peculiar Aussie twang, the unspoilt, virgin beaches and the magnificent and rugged landscapes. Within months of 'Hoges' appearing on US television screens, Australia became a 'must-see' destination, rocketing from number seventy-eight to number seven on the most-desired holiday list. There were 70,000 inquiries from Americans in that period alone! The timing could not have been better. Airfares were becoming more affordable and the Australian dollar was low. Almost overnight, 'Down Under' became the world's hottest destination.

The most admirable part was that Paul Hogan didn't make a single dollar for appearing in the iconic ad, donating all his earnings to charity instead. Now that's very Australian, most Australians would be quick to admit!

As the aircraft began the descent into Kuala Lumpur, Elise woke up as if on cue. Having first checked on her husband Jack and ensuring he was strapped in for the landing, she returned, looking at us blankly as if trying to pick up the thread of our earlier conversation. Ambika and I acted busy, rearranging our trays and seats. As we landed and taxied to the designated bay, Elise suddenly remembered that she had been educating us on the perennial dangers lurking in Australia. Just as we were exiting the aircraft, she shot off one final warning to Ambika.

'Beware of the box jellyfish! I've heard that their sting is excruciating and in extreme cases can cause death. The most lethal poison known to mankind, I'm told.' With that parting gesture, she strolled away, grasping Jack's arm as he meekly followed her down the aisle, resigned, I expect, to his fate.

CHAPTER 3
Two Backpacks and a Business Suit

All that is gold does not glitter, not all those who wander are lost – J.R.R. Tolkien

The second leg of our journey, from Kuala Lumpur to Brisbane, was more relaxed than the first. After take-off, we moved to an empty row of seats at the rear of the plane. Ambika was quick to take the window seat, eager to get a glimpse of the Australian continent as we entered Australian airspace. The aircraft was navigating a circular route that met the Australian coast somewhere near the Mitchell Plateau in the Kimberley region of Western Australia. Although we were thirty-five thousand feet in the air, we could see the land very clearly, the red earth contrasting sharply against the strikingly azure skies. The rugged plains seemed to stretch on forever.

Although the land below us appeared flat and featureless, below the earth's surface the land was bursting with an abundance of natural wealth. Australia's natural resources are legendary; iron ore of the highest grade (which incidentally gave the soil the characteristic ochre colour), gold, nickel and a plethora of mineral deposits of unimaginable value abound. Of particular interest to Ambika, having worked in the diamond industry, was the Argyle mine, producer of the famous pink 'Kimberley' diamonds.

The mine has been operating since 1983 and has produced more than 800 million carats of rough diamonds. So rich is the bounty that during early exploration in the 1970s, creek prospecting yielded whole, fist-sized crystals, with one team finding no fewer than *fifteen* large and precious rocks in their sieve pan. I watched Ambika as she sat straining at her seat, nose pressed to the plexiglass window hoping to catch a glimpse of some of that dazzle and sparkle.

I'd imagined landing in Brisbane to rousing applause and a cacophony of cheers from the Australian immigration welcoming committee. There would be rainbow-coloured streamers flying in the air, party poppers going off and cheerleaders with pom-poms gesticulating wildly with choreographed precision. Understandably, nothing like this occurred. We were just two new migrants amid the constant stream who made the move to Australia every year. This did not dampen our spirits one bit, though. We were elated to have finally arrived. It marked the culmination of a year's worth of planning, hard work and sacrifice.

The most terrifying part for many new arrivals is the strict Australian quarantine and border protection agencies who keep a close eye on all inbound visitors. Having watched the *Border Security* series on TV, we had come well prepared. Ambika had spent an entire day before we left fastidiously scrubbing the soles of all our shoes of stray dirt or debris until they were as good as new. The arrival passenger card was detailed and half the questions related to the declaration of food items, animal products and any interaction with flora and fauna overseas one might have had. It seemed like overkill, but being geographically isolated Australia has very few diseases and agricultural pests. As such, defences must be bolstered in every possible way.

Australia has one of the world's most, if not *the* most, strict quarantine programs for all imports. Even within the country, certain food items are not allowed to be transferred from one state to another. Breaking quarantine laws is taken very seriously indeed. Any invasive species, of which Australia has seen more than its fair share, represents a threat and potentially a significant drain on the economy. Worse still, it can cause catastrophic and often irreversible damage to the native flora and fauna.

Take the case of the common red ant (European fire ant). Since 2000, there have been four red ant incursions detected and, according to one estimate, the Australian government has spent more than $300 million trying to get rid of them. Evidence suggests this species found its way into Australia through goods transported on ships. Red ants have more ecological impacts than other ants because they can reach incredibly high densities of up to 2600 mounds per hectare. I don't know how much that equates to in ant-terms, but it does seem like an awful lot, especially when you consider the fact that they damage crops by the acre, rob beehives, harm young domestic animals and destroy infrastructure. They also have a mean sting which can cause death. Something our erstwhile travelling companion Elise failed to mention!

As we stood in the queue at Brisbane airport, a stocky, taciturn quarantine official dressed in a crisp black uniform with a matching baseball cap was examining the bags of an Asian couple ahead of us. With latex gloves on, the official inspected the contents of one of the bags with the clinical curiosity of a coroner conducting an autopsy. She was soon rewarded with a bag of contraband red chillies. After a few pointed questions from the official and a lot of hand gesturing from the visitors, the official unceremoniously dumped the chillies in the bin. She then hefted the couple's bag off the counter, motioning them to proceed to the exit. We fared much better and with just a cursory glance and a few routine questions we were ushered through.

In the arrivals hall, we were welcomed by Ambika's relatives, Nelson and Asha (*sans* pom-poms). Asha had a chirpy disposition and every time she smiled, her face radiated merriment. She had moved to Australia after her recent marriage. Her husband, Nelson, however, had migrated to New Zealand nearly a decade ago. Sensing more opportunities 'across the ditch', he'd moved to Australia and established a thriving education business. Of medium height and built like an oak, he exuded a sense of calm. The generous couple opened their home to us and graciously let us use their house as a staging area/storage bay to plan our forthcoming backpacking adventure. They even offered to allow us to leave any excess baggage with them while we were on the road.

It was just past eight at night as the taxi took us to the suburb where they lived. The first thing that struck us was the silence. For a moment I thought that all the residents had locked up and left on an annual holiday. Nelson pointed out that it was already bedtime for most families and the peace and quiet was normal for this time of the night. We had just arrived from Mumbai, a throbbing megapolis known as 'Maximum City' which took pride in the fact that it never slept. Winding down at 8 p.m. every night would take a little getting used to.

The couple lived in a beautiful three-bedroom brick house in a quiet leafy suburb just a few kilometres from the airport. It was an average dwelling by Australian standards – but very spacious by world standards – and had been recently refurbished. The living room opened on to an undercover sun deck which housed a barbecue and an outdoor table and chairs. My heart was already welling with hope, watching Nelson, a migrant just like me, enjoying such a beautiful house and a comfortable lifestyle. It was something that seemed within the grasp of most people in Australia. Nelson said that many migrants who arrived with nothing were able to achieve a decent lifestyle within a few years.

Our first full day 'Down Under' was spent prepping for our trip. We left most of our clothes and non-essential gear in two big suitcases with Nelson and Asha. One peculiar addition was a wheelie bag containing our documents – academic qualifications, resumés, and details of our professional achievements. The kit also held our business suits in the hope we might snare an interview (and possibly a job opening) while travelling. We were backpackers out to explore all that Australia had to offer – but we were also newly arrived migrants ultimately in search of jobs.

Although Ambika and I had both done a fair bit of travelling, this journey was different for many reasons. It was a pleasure trip in a foreign land, an initiation trip in our adopted country, and a road trip for networking. It was also an opportunity to experience the culture and ethos of Australia and its people first-hand before settling down. We were determined to enjoy our time and fully 'buy into' the culture. All we needed now was to figure out which way we were headed.

CHAPTER 4
A River Runs Through It

I don't know where I'm going, but I promise it won't be boring – David Bowie

Nelson and Asha were extremely accommodating and offered to let us stay for as long as we needed. However, we were mindful of stretching the friendship and didn't want to impose so we booked into an Airbnb apartment in a charming, inner-city suburb named Clayfield, about twenty minutes' drive from the city. Nelson and Asha drove us there, wondering how we came to be staying with strangers given we'd only just landed in the country.

This was 2014 and the world was slowly waking up to the 'home share' concept. With the benefit of hindsight, there was a void in the tourism industry that no one knew existed until Airbnb came along. This online service platform has given the power back to travellers who now have endless accommodation options besides dingy hostels or overpriced hotels and resorts. For property owners, Airbnb represented a fantastic opportunity to make money from a fixed asset. For travellers, you could save a lot and find something that precisely suited your needs and comfort levels, a real Godsend for cash-strapped backpackers. Another outcome, which appealed to us, was the social aspect – the opportunity to make friends from a myriad of countries, ethnicities and cultures.

It's remarkable the concept got off the ground at all. Like most success stories, the Airbnb concept evolved out of sheer necessity. Two roommates Brian Chesky and Joe Gebbia had just moved to San Francisco in 2007 and were struggling to make ends meet. At one stage, the cash-strapped duo were in such dire straits that they were unable to cough up enough money to cover their rent. Out of this undesirable situation was born an ingenious concept. Brian and Joe came up with the idea of putting an inflatable mattress in their living room and renting it out. The goal at first was 'to make a few bucks'. They had no idea how big this business would eventually become.

The platform offers not only beds and rooms but a host of other homestay options as well, from the very basic to the downright exotic: entire apartments and homes, castles, boats, manors, tree houses, igloos and even islands. We would have loved to have been able to rent an island, but we were on a budget and so had to temper our aspirations. In the end, the only places we did not use Airbnb were Melbourne and Sydney, which was purely out of convenience, as we wanted to be in the heart of these cities, close to the action. On those occasions, we opted for hostels (a whole new experience for us as well).

Anna's Airbnb apartment was on the top floor of a three-storey block. It was compact yet breezy with a kitchen flowing into the main dining area and living space. Our room was small but equipped with a queen-size bed, a large built-in wardrobe and a small window set high up on the wall. The toilet and shower facilities were just across the hallway and were for guests' use only. The living room, dining and kitchen facilities, however, were shared with our host. In her twenties, Anna was studying for a Masters in Dietetics at Queensland University while working part-time at a local salon. She was a late-nighter who preferred to study way past midnight and then sleep in when she wasn't working. This arrangement worked out well for us as it meant we had the shared spaces mostly to ourselves during the day.

A second generation Australian, Anna hadn't travelled much outside of Australia and found our life story fascinating. She was intrigued to hear of our grand plans and commended us for doing something so bold.

'Have you decided where you're going to settle down?' she asked. 'I highly recommend Brisbane. Don't fall for all the hype surrounding Sydney or Melbourne. They're overcrowded, expensive and the traffic is horrendous. Besides, the weather's better here. Queensland isn't called the "Sunshine State" for nothing. We're also the reigning NRL (National Rugby League) champions.'

We soon learnt Australians were immensely proud of their home states and took every opportunity to take friendly jibes at their counterparts across the border. This was also a sports-crazy nation, and if we were to live here, we'd not only have to swear allegiance to a game but also a team. It would all depend on which city we finally settled in, so we were not judged too harshly just yet.

'We have no clue where we'll settle,' Ambika replied. 'The reality we face as migrants is that we will go where the job takes us, and we may not have a choice in the matter.'

Ambika was right. Most migrants made a beeline for Sydney and Melbourne as that's where the jobs were. It would have been easier if we were seeking work in mainstream industries like IT, media, banking or retail. Ambika had a business degree and years of experience in the retail and media sectors and could easily have found a mid-management role in the major cities. I, on the other hand, had limited choices due to my specific marine skillset and this meant we'd more than likely end up at some remote port town along the vast coastline. It was a conscious decision on our part that I would be the primary provider as we had yet to start a family and once kids came along, Ambika would most probably have to quit her job and be a stay-at-home mum for a while.

'As of now we're living in a zone of uncertainty,' I said. 'We're not sure how to apply for a job and we have no networks to tap into. We're also still learning the basics – how to rent an apartment, the cost of groceries, and how much our daily expenses will be.'

'Don't worry,' Anna replied, hoping to boost our morale, 'your story reminds me of my parents who migrated from the UK decades ago. They faced struggles and hardships when they first got here but within a couple of years Dad had not only found a great job but in no time rose to the level of manager. They bought a house and were in quite a happy place. They don't call this the "lucky country" for nothing.'

Anna made a good point. Stories of migrants arriving with nothing but a few meagre possessions, facing innumerable challenges, working hard and eventually succeeding was the dominant theme for many people we met during our journey. Ultimately, it was such invaluable insights that gave us the heart to persevere when we faced our own struggles.

'Just don't settle in New South Wales or Victoria,' Anna reminded us. 'You'll be hard-pressed to find friendlier communities outside of Queensland.'

Over the next few days we registered for Medicare cards, opened bank accounts, and applied for debit cards. I began investigating the job market but soon realised my overseas work experience might not count for much. The biggest hurdle I faced was that I had no specific 'Australian experience', a difficult thing to achieve considering I'd only just arrived.

'A common problem we all faced when we first got here,' Nelson said matter-of-factly when we caught up for dinner. 'I recommend you start connecting with people within your industry, brush up your resume and just focus on getting your name out there.'

And that's precisely what I did. I worked in the pre-dawn darkness and late at night, honing my CV, gathering contact details of maritime companies and reaching out to my peers and industry seniors. Although there were no specific offers, the positive outcome of all those cold calls and emails was that people were prepared to listen. Being a country of migrants, it seemed they instinctively understood our challenges. The more calls I made, the more networking opportunities arose, and soon word got out that I was available to join at short notice and ready to relocate if a suitable opportunity presented itself.

We developed an excellent battle rhythm during our stay at Anna's – wake at 5 a.m., work on resumés, surf job portals and make a list of prospective employers. Around mid-morning, we would go and explore the city, returning late in the evening. We would then dedicate an hour or so to our travel plans and make all the necessary bookings. Each night we crashed into bed utterly exhausted. But not before praying that we would stay safe, have the grace to make the right decisions and the good fortune to be guided in the right direction.

CHAPTER 5
Of Strange Beasts and Distant Lands

Remember, this is the country of the duck-billed platypus. When you are cut off from the rest of the world, things are bound to develop in interesting ways – Peter Carey, My Life as a Fake

What Brisbane may lack in surf and beaches, it more than makes up for in the form of its beautiful, undulating waterway – the Brisbane River. The longest in south-east Queensland, it begins life in the Great Dividing Range, nearly 200 kilometres north-west of the capital. It then flows eastward, snaking through Brisbane's western suburbs with funny-sounding jingling names like Jindalee, Indooroopilly and Toowong. At the lower reaches, it eventually spills into Moreton Bay, a vast and environmentally sensitive expanse of water flanked by Moreton Island to the east.

Both the river and the chance of establishing a colony were missed by at least four early explorers, including Captain Cook, who visited Moreton Bay but failed to discover the mouth of the river. If not for a group of ticket-of-leave convicts, Thomas Pamphlett, John Finnegan, Richard Parsons and John Thompson, Brisbane may never have been born. After setting off from Sydney in a 29-foot boat in March 1823 with the intention of travelling south, the group somehow drifted north, where they were hit by ferocious gales and forced to spend some twenty-four days lost at sea. Out of provisions and drinking water, Thompson fell ill and died, while the other three barely made it ashore. Having lost all hope of returning to Sydney, they wandered inland and stumbled upon the river purely by chance.

While Parsons continued travelling further north, Pamphlett and Finnegan stayed and lived with the local Indigenous community for nearly eight months until John Oxley, the Surveyor-General of New South Wales, sailed up the coast and into Moreton Bay looking for a new site for a convict settlement. On 2 December 1823, with John Finnegan's help, he entered what would become known as the Brisbane River. Proceeding upstream, Oxley noted the abundant fish and tall pine trees and marvelled at the sheer natural beauty of the place. Based on his survey, a colony was soon established on the riverbank.

More than 450 miles from Sydney, Brisbane was initially earmarked for the really 'bad boys' – those recidivist convicts who were deemed worthy of even *more* punishment – and it soon garnered a reputation as one of the harshest penal settlements in the land. The convict era, however, was slowly coming to an end and by the 1830s, 'free settlers' had begun to arrive. With the increased number of new arrivals, there was considerable pressure to allow them to live in the new northern colony.

According to the 1825 census, Brisbane's population consisted of forty-five male convicts and two female convicts. Today, it's a world-class metropolis with a population of nearly 2.5 million. It boasts many prominent cultural institutions, including a remarkable modern art gallery (GOMA) and a vibrant theatre precinct (QPAC). In addition, Brisbane has hosted the 1982 Commonwealth Games, World Expo 88 and the 2014 G20 summit.

The city that Ambika and I beheld that bright August morning was a far cry from the tough penal settlement of nearly two centuries earlier. As we left the central railway station, people from different walks of life, cultures and races raced past us. Business executives in expensive suits and tanned leather bags, college students with noise-cancelling headphones and loose jumpers, office employees in smart casuals and polished footwear, school kids wearing the bright colours of their respective alma maters, and hordes of tourists just like us. We ambled along the Queen Street Mall, a vibrant shopping and lifestyle pedestrian precinct at the heart of the city. The Mall featured a melange of boutique retail stores, international fashion brands, souvenir shops, expensive restaurants, lively cafés and convenience stores. In the centre of the mall was a low-rise stage which was used to promote local artists and performers. It was hard not to get caught up in the revelry and the convivial spirit of the place.

We had our first Australian picnic lunch in Anzac Square, a small patch of manicured lawn in the centre of the business district overlooking the Anzac Memorial. The city council initiative of providing recliner chairs in the square for general use added a nice touch to the beautiful setting. Tall office buildings with gleaming glass façades reflecting the bright morning sun towered around us in all directions. In between sat colonial-era sandstone and brick buildings, creating a classic blend of new-age modernism and age-old character. The numerous gardens purposefully positioned amid the office blocks offered pleasant respite and was a testimony to the vision of the founding fathers. This was a city built not just with functionality in mind, but with a sense of civic pride and aesthetics.

Part of me was viewing Brisbane through the eyes of a short-term visitor, admiring the clean streets, the glamorous storefronts and the bustling cafés and bars. But another part of me was trying to picture living here – discussing local events and cheering for the local footy team at the pub with my office mates after a busy day. This was our home now, and if things went to plan, we'd be Australian citizens within a few years.

Later in the afternoon, we wandered past Brisbane City Hall, the imposing granite edifice built in the Italian Renaissance style which dominates King George Square. Two life-sized bronze lions, modelled on the lions in Trafalgar Square in London, stand guard at the entrance, while a regal statue of King George V sits proudly on a horse in one corner, a tribute from the citizens of Brisbane. Atop the main structure, like a giant sail mast, is a 70-metre-high clock tower which is based on the St Mark's campanile in Venice. When it was first constructed, the four clock faces on each side of the tower were the largest in Australia. The clock even had Westminster chimes which sounded on the quarter-hour. The city hall design, the bronze lions, the statue of the King and the details of the clock down to the distinctive chime evidenced the deep longing felt by those early settlers for Great Britain, a country they still thought of as home.

We continued exploring the city for the remainder of the afternoon, drifting like a rudderless boat, following the course of the river as it took dramatic hairpin turns, the curved banks revealing the city's best entertainment spots to us bit by bit. The free hop on-hop off service on the inner-city buses and the CityHopper ferry provided us the freedom and mobility to explore the town with leisure. The spectacular South Bank foreshore with its 42 acres of lush parklands, world-class eateries and stunning river views gives this part of town a perpetual holiday vibe. Australians love their beaches and so the innovative Brisbanites overcame their lack of an oceanfront by creating a man-made beach in the heart of the city. The aptly named Streets Beach features a stunning lagoon surrounded by white sands and sub-tropical plants.

To our minds, however, the best feature of this beautiful city is the sprawling riverside City Botanic Gardens which create a serene backdrop for the undulating river, with ancient cycads, palms and fig trees crowding the water's edge. Covering some 49 acres, the gardens provide a welcome respite to locals and visitors alike. The early settlers had undoubtedly got this one right – nurturing and preserving plant species for future generations despite the hardships faced during those early days would have been difficult. In part, this was no doubt driven by their desire to create an environment that resembled England.

While in Brisbane we made a day trip to the Lone Pine Koala Sanctuary, a world-class facility located around 13 kilometres from the city. Up until our arrival, we had only heard of the country's exotic and peculiar animals. It was time to get personal and the sanctuary provided us with a safe and controlled introduction. To be honest, after Elise's warnings, we were dreading a chance encounter with Australian wildlife once we were on the road, no matter how cute and harmless they might appear.

Officially recognised by the *Guinness World Records* book, the sanctuary is the world's first and largest koala park, housing nearly a hundred and thirty of these cute and cuddly furballs. It's also home to kangaroos and a wide variety of other Australian wildlife – wombats, Tasmanian devils, echidnas, cassowaries, platypus, possums and emus. People from all over the world – and we were no exception – line up dutifully to cuddle the cute koalas, feed the shy kangaroos and pat the wallabies.

The animals on display were but a small representation of the immense diversity of Australia's flora and fauna. Home to over a million individual species, around 80 per cent of Australia's plants, mammals, reptiles and frogs are found nowhere else on the planet. A staggering statistic that was also one of the country's most appealing characteristics. What was even more astounding was that new species were being discovered every single day.

How did such diversity evolve? Most of the country's peculiarities stem from one overarching historical feature – prolonged isolation. Until the chance discovery of the continent by Europeans in the seventeenth century, much of the world didn't even know that Australia existed. For millions of years, the landmass was so far removed from any other that plants and animals had no interaction with other species. Separation of the landmasses began about 180 million years ago, in the Jurassic period, when the western half of Gondwana (which included Africa and South America) detached from the eastern half (which included Madagascar, India, Australia and Antarctica). Then about 140 million years ago, Africa detached from South America and the South Atlantic Ocean started forming. Around the same time, India separated from Antarctica and Australia, creating the Indian Ocean. India continued to drift north, eventually head-butting the Asian continent, creating the majestic Himalayan range of mountains in the process.

Meanwhile, Australia drifted lazily to the furthest corner of the world; unspoilt and untouched, separated by vast swirling oceans, its isolation complete. This created habitats and animals of the most peculiar dispositions.

The other continents stayed relatively close to each other and, over time, collided or joined parts of the old Laurasia landmass. These cross-border interactions affected the animal species in their race for survival. Monotremes (platypus and echidnas – egg-laying mammals that feed their babies with milk) and marsupials (kangaroos and wallabies – animals that carry their young in a pouch) were unable to compete with the more advanced placental mammals (cattle, sheep, horses and elephants) and became mostly extinct.

In Australia, however, the reverse unfolded.

The climate on the continent had changed, becoming drier. Monotremes and marsupials, with their less demanding reproductive systems, were more suited to this new environment and became the dominant fauna. What remaining placental animals that had survived slowly died out.

Today, Australia is the only continent in the world to still have all three of the major groups of mammals. It's also the only continent other than Antarctica that has no native hoofed animals or terrestrial carnivores. The dingo or wild dog is the largest carnivorous mammal – a far cry from the majestic lions, tigers and elephants that inhabit the land where Ambika and I come from! But don't for a minute think you're safe in Australia: consider the lethal sting of the deceptively tiny jellyfish, or the toxic venom of innumerable native snakes and spiders. What these creatures lack in size, they more than make up for in terms of their ability to inflict suffering. Indeed, the amount of toxicity contained in one single bite or sting seems wildly excessive for animals that evolved in isolation. Take, for example, the inland taipan, ranked as the most venomous snake in the world. Why would a reclusive creature that lives in the remote, rocky habitat of the outback need venom so potent that it could easily kill a hundred men with a single strike? Even from a predatory perspective, the taipan has 40,000 times more venom than it needs to kill its common prey, the long-haired rat! Yeah, this is a peculiar country indeed.

After having spent the entire day at the sanctuary we were exhausted with the excursion but equally thrilled to have finally seen some of the most peculiar species from Down Under.

On our final weekend in Brisbane, Nelson and Asha drove us to Redcliffe, a charming coastal suburb about 30 kilometres north of the city, famous for its great farmer's market. Music lovers would also know that Redcliffe was once 'home' to the world-famous pop group, the Bee Gees. Over four decades the group produced hit after hit, selling more than 200 million albums. The local council has renamed an alley in their honour, converting it into an open-air walkthrough with a museum featuring legendary stories, life-size statues and snippets from the lives of brothers Barry, Robin and Maurice Gibb.

The weekend markets were sprawled along Redcliffe Parade just metres from gourmet restaurants, cafés, bistros and bars. This offered locals and tourists the best of both worlds – leisurely brunches with spectacular views and the opportunity to buy fresh farm produce at competitive prices. The markets also offered arts and crafts, jewellery, clothing, children's toys, exotic imports, ethnic foods and live entertainment. We devoured some of the most delicious pancakes at Pappy's, a food cart managed by a lovely retired couple who operated the business purely out of passion. Quite a task, if you ask me, having to wake up at 3 a.m. on the weekend, load up the mobile cart, drive for an hour and set up shop. Only to do it all again the following weekend! But the couple clearly derived immense pleasure from this activity. They served their food with love and this was reflected in the long queue of patient patrons outside their cart.

We strolled around the markets while Asha bought her weekly supply of groceries. From bush honey to handcrafted amulets, custom-made chopping boards to fresh pawpaws from the hinterland, the markets overflowed with wonderful local produce and handicrafts. Ambika and I got caught up in the palpable feeling of bonhomie and thought to ourselves that this was a lifestyle we could get used to.

When I was a little boy, my nanna would take my sister and me to the weekend markets in what was then known as Bombay. Vegetable vendors, trinket sellers and wholesale merchants would flood the streets with their carts, competing to woo customers. The heady smell of exotic spices suffused the air, and the cacophony of trade was almost like a physical force that threatened to knock you over. The markets would spill over into the nearby fish market where the women of the fishing community would squat in a neat row, selling the catch of the day, fresh off the boat. Nanna had a well-rehearsed circuit – buy vegetables; haggle with the fishmonger; go to the butcher's shop, haggle some more; pick up all the weekly groceries and, once done, indulge her grandchildren with some trinkets, a piece of candy or an ice-cream.

Clutching Nanna's hand tightly, my sister and I would gawk at the scale of the bazaar, the number of people and the incessant din. But then, over time, the city just seemed to implode under its own weight. The local municipality reclaimed the marketplace to widen the roads and make way for future expansions. Our weekend routine became a distant memory. Experiencing the markets in Redcliffe awakened dormant memories and I was transported back to my childhood where all I needed to make me happy was a popsicle and a bouncing yo-yo.

After our week in Brisbane, it was time to move on to our next destination – the Sunshine Coast. Nelson dropped us at the train station, and we bid our farewells, promising to return to collect our baggage. Hopefully, by then, we'd be closer to finding a job and a suitable city in which to settle down.

As we boarded the northbound train at Toombul Station, we felt as though we were stepping into the realm of the unknown. In Brisbane, we had the comfort of having familiar faces around, and everything seemed safe and manageable. Would we soon be frolicking with a school of dolphins in the turquoise sea, or would we find ourselves stranded on a forlorn reef, miles from civilisation? Would we be chasing colourful butterflies in lush rainforests, or would we be chased by hungry crocodiles? Would we run out of money midway through our trip, or would we have the most memorable experiences of our lives? Only the journey ahead would tell.

CHAPTER 6
Heads we go North!

A journey is like marriage. The certain way to be wrong is to think you control it – John Steinbeck

The story goes that Queensland's Sunshine Coast got its name after a group of local real estate agents gathered one balmy tropical afternoon at the Caloundra Hotel and endlessly, thoroughly and conscientiously debated the issue until a suitable moniker was chosen. Others claim that it was just a casual catch-up and the agents came up with the name in no time at all – and then spent the rest of the night celebrating with endless rounds of beer. Everyone, however, agrees that the name change was a resounding and instant success and helped to revive the region's slumping economy.

The year was 1958 and Queensland was falling behind the other states. In Victoria, Melbourne had just triumphantly hosted the 1956 Summer Olympics, the first time the event had been held in the southern hemisphere. Meanwhile in New South Wales, Sydney was about to embark on yet another grand project – the construction of Sydney Opera House, a mammoth endeavour that was certain to shift the spotlight back onto the country's first city. At almost 10 million, Australia's population was growing, but only 14 per cent of this number lived in Queensland. Queensland needed to act and act fast if it were to shake off its image of being an easy-going and sleepy borough, great for a short-term holiday but not for setting up a home or investment.

I can just imagine those estate agents discussing these challenges, trying to devise a strategy to make their region more attractive. The problem, they might have concluded (after a few rounds of beers), was simple: their town's name was terrible. Who'd want to visit a place called 'Near North Coast'? So what if the region boasted miles of virgin beaches fringed with swaying palms in the front yard and pristine, unspoilt rainforests in the backyard? 'Near North Coast' did not have an inspiring ring to it. You can just picture mums and dads back then planning the school holidays.

'Honey, where do you think we should go this time?' asks Mum.

'Why, let's make a trip to … the Near North Coast,' answers Dad. 'It's got some lovely beaches, I hear.'

'And where exactly is this Near North Coast?' Mum asks.

'Dunno … somewhere north of Brisbane, I guess.'

Back at the Caloundra Hotel, the day dragged on with little progress. But then someone had an idea. Just south of Brisbane, the recently renamed 'Gold Coast' had seen a big rise in visitor numbers. 'Gold' sounded great; *that* was somewhere people wanted to visit. Following more rounds of beers, scores of suggestions and a long drawn discussion, the name 'Sunshine Coast' was mooted. It suited the character of the place. It had an inspirational ring to it. After a lot of back-thumping (and no doubt more rounds of beers), Near North Coast was unofficially rechristened.

Rechristening a town doesn't happen overnight, however, and for years nothing changed. Finally, in November 1966, some eight sunny summers after that folkloric gathering at the Caloundra Hotel, the local shires voted to approve the new name and 'Sunshine Coast' was officially reborn. The benefits were significant and, in seemingly no time at all, the sleepy little farming towns known mainly for pineapples and sugar cane evolved into one of Australia's most popular holiday destinations for both local and overseas tourists alike. Today, nearly three million people visit every year, and the Sunshine Coast has become the third most populated area in Queensland.

Ambika and I chose the Sunshine Coast over the Gold Coast as our next port of call because most of the travel books we consulted tended to depict the latter as a glitzy sort of place with larger-than-life theme parks (perfect for families with kids) and a groovy, vibrant nightlife (ideal for party-goers and night-clubbers). We didn't fall into either category and much preferred what the Sunshine Coast offered – tranquil beaches and quiet, leafy suburbs. We were past the age of partying and binge-drinking and, truth be told, neither of us had ever really related to that sort of lifestyle. We preferred walks in nature and untamed adventure over rock concerts and midnight cocktails. I guess some matches really are made in heaven!

As the train snaked its way out of Brisbane, the landscape changed almost instantaneously. Houses gave way to large acreages, drooping eucalypts and exotic pines. The undulating peaks of the Glass House Mountains slid by as if in slow motion. These majestic ranges were named by Captain Cook in 1770 as their shape reminded him of the glass furnaces in his native Yorkshire. They just looked like regular mountain peaks to me, but then, to be fair, I had never seen the glass furnaces in Yorkshire.

We alighted at Landsborough, a sleepy little suburb in the Sunshine Coast hinterland, and boarded the city bus which would take us to our next connection. The iconic Australia Zoo, made famous by Steve Irwin, lay just a few kilometres south. Throughout the 1990s and early 2000s, Steve Irwin brought the Australian outdoors into the living rooms of millions of people around the world. Although known for his high-octane energy and characteristic Australian twang, he was also a passionate and enthusiastic conservationist and a staunch wildlife advocate. Tragically, he died prematurely at just forty-four years of age in 2006 while filming a documentary. Today, his family carry on his work running the zoo. Having already visited the Lone Pine Sanctuary and got our fill of native fauna for the time being, we decided to give the Australia Zoo a miss. The uncharted road beckoned us, and we had faraway places to explore, unspoilt beaches to visit and scores of new friends to make.

Two bus connections and a further hour's journey later, we reached the coastal suburb of Bokarina at the southern end of the Sunshine Coast. We walked the last kilometre to our next Airbnb: Helen's beach villa. We chose the villa because of its secluded location and proximity to the coast and town.

Backed by the meandering Mooloolah River, Bokarina offers a world-class waterway with million-dollar waterfront homes dotting the lagoon, most with their private jetties. Boating, paddling and kayaking are just some of the activities available; if so inclined, you can even take a river cruise to gawk at the flash houses that line the foreshores. This was a lifestyle far removed from the one Ambika and I were used to in India.

We had spoken to our host Helen briefly over the phone seeking directions after we got off the bus and she was expecting us. As we arrived at her villa, as if on cue the wrought-iron gates rolled open. Two stout stone gargoyles sat on either side atop the gateposts, their grotesque faces and scaly wings at odds with the tranquil surroundings. The white-pebbled driveway was gleaming in the afternoon sun, and the compact front garden was bursting with an abundance of native and exotic plants. A white pergola provided a stunning contrast to the profusion of greenery. Native plant vines, waify grass, fuchsias and coast palm lilies filled the garden space. The garden had a colourful array of garden gnomes and tastefully chosen bric-a-brac. A three-tiered birdbath with a recirculating fountain added a zen-like serenity.

Helen was a small woman in her early sixties, slim, with blonde hair, intense grey eyes and a charming persona that could put anyone at ease. She was one of those people who aged gracefully. Her age was masked by her enthusiasm which would have put an average twenty year old to shame. Hot on her heels were two cute and spirited Maltese Shitzu dogs named Pugget and Happy who wasted no time doing the customary dog-sniffing at our feet and around our bags, voting their approval for us to enter. Helen greeted us with a warm hug. Noticing our backpacks and wheelie bag, she remarked jokingly, 'You guys seem packed to live here for a month! Are you sure you're staying for only three nights?'

After assuring her our plans hadn't changed, Helen showed us around her house. It had an open-plan layout with whites dominating the walls, floors and kitchen. This served as the perfect backdrop for displaying her numerous artefacts, paintings and handmade trinkets. It was clear that Helen was a prolific traveller and an avid art collector, but this was just a fraction of her real depth. Renovating, landscaping, gardening, crafting handmade leather bags, writing children's stories and poetry were some of her other interests. Most of the handcrafted creations were designed by Helen herself, a small measure of her bursting creativity and relentless energy. By her own admission, she made little money from any of her crafts; she did it purely out of an eagerness to learn and to grow. And as if all of this weren't enough, she hosted Airbnb guests because it provided her with an opportunity to make new friends and to learn about new cultures.

Helen was a first-generation migrant who'd moved to Australia from London in the 1970s. In her early twenties, she'd bought a 'Ten Pound Pom' ticket but due to the untimely death of her father, she was unable to travel at that time. Her dream to migrate might have fizzled had it not been for a chance encounter at a pub. Out on a boring date one night, Helen drifted away from her partner and went to the bar. The young barmaid who served her turned out to be an Australian – the first Helen had ever met – and the girls hit it off almost instantly. Helen's dreams of migrating to Australia were rekindled and, soon after, with just £300 in her pocket, she moved to Sydney to start a new life. Australia exceeded her expectations: she was captivated by the unspoilt beauty, the wealth of opportunity and the genuineness and warmth of the people. She only returned occasionally to the UK for the odd holiday to see family and friends.

The 'Ten Pound Pom' campaign was a well-packaged campaign run jointly by the British and Australian governments between 1945 and 1972 with the aim of boosting Australia's population. World War II was just over and Britain was a depressing place. Many of its citizens were seeking a way out, hoping to find better living conditions elsewhere. Australia, on the other hand, needed more people to help build its economy. The frontier colony, although full of potential, was doomed to collapse if timely remedial action was not affected. The 'White Australia' policy was still in force at the time, and the resultant imbalance worked perfectly for both governments: one was glad to ship people off in the thousands while the other was eager to welcome them.

The marketing strategy was simple. Offered what was known as an 'assisted passage' Britons were sold dreams of a better life and a brighter future in Australia. The average cost was about £120 but the Australian Government-subsidised £110 of this amount which meant the immigrants paid only £10 for a one-way ticket. Children received free berthage. On the face of it, it was a good deal, and in no time at all the phones of the shipping offices were ringing off the hook. People clambered over each other, eager to set sail for this strange, beguiling land on the other side of the world.

It was anticipated some 70,000 Britons a year would make the long voyage to Australia, but in the first year alone, around 400,000 people applied. There was one disclaimer in small print which most passengers consciously chose to ignore: you had to stay for a minimum of two years or pay the full return fare back to Great Britain, a lot of money in those days. During the 1950s and 1960s, around a million Britons emigrated under the scheme. Some did return, though – around 250,000 during the life of the campaign – and those who stayed called them 'whinging poms', much to their displeasure. The new arrivals soon discovered most Australian cities and towns were little more than fledging outposts and housing and employment were hard to come by. For those who chose to remain, however, there were immense rewards to be reaped, as there were opportunities everywhere. Once you found a job, many immigrants were able to save enough to buy a decent-sized parcel of land. Famous Australians associated with the 'Ten Pound Pom' scheme include former Australian Prime Minister Julia Gillard, the Gibb brothers (of the Bee Gees fame), and entertainers Kylie Minogue and Hugh Jackman. Not a bad influx of talent for £10, one would have to agree.

Heads we go North!

Back in Bokarina, Helen showed us to our room which was tucked away in the far end of the house, a respectful distance from the main living area and other bedrooms. The rest of the house, including the kitchen, were shared. Helen left us to our own devices and handed us the house keys and the garage remote.

We dumped our bags and rushed out the door like two excited kids, eager to get our first glimpse of an Australian beach. We cut across the short stretch of coastal parkland, an area dominated by tall eucalypts, expansive screw pines and droopy casuarinas. As soon as we cleared the coastal vegetation, we were rewarded with glorious views of the Coral Sea, a shock of deep blue beneath an equally blue sky. The beach was quiet at that time of the day and we sat on one of the park benches perched high on the edge of the path which offered a good vantage point.

A strong north-easterly whipped up the waves and the late August chill still had a decent bite to it. Before us, the beach stretched for nearly two kilometres from the Point Cartwright headland in the north to the Currimundi Lake in the south. The secluded spot, the swish-swash of the swaying casuarinas, the warmth of the sun in sharp contrast to the winter chill made for the perfect occasion for idle musings. Ambika and I sat together in silence, enjoying the moment, happy to drift in the direction of our own thoughts, yet firmly linked to each other by an invisible thread. I wondered if we would have developed this chemistry in such a short amount of time if we were living the average life of a house-and-career-bound couple. I felt lucky to have experienced life on the road before I met my soulmate. And even luckier to have met someone who shared my love for travel and with whom I now looked forward to sharing all my future adventures. In the immortal words of the American author Robert Brault, 'What we find in a soulmate is not something wild to tame, but something wild to run with.'

CHAPTER 7
Sea Creatures

Everything I was I carry with me, everything I will be lies waiting on the road ahead – Ma Jian, Red Dust: A Path Through China

That evening, we met Ann, Helen's sister, who was recuperating from a recent stroke. Ann's surgeon had suggested mental stimuli in the form of puzzles or crosswords to reconfigure her neural pathways and accelerate her healing. Fiercely independent, Ann would come home every night after work and challenge herself with these puzzles. This was our first experience of an endearing Australian trait – the ability to get up when life knocked you down, brush the dirt off your knees and move on. No tears, no sympathy, no calls for help. The most sentiment that was allowed, it would appear, was to merely shrug your shoulders and get on with life. I suspected this attitude stemmed from two centuries of hardship and daily struggle, often in the face of isolation from other communities being established elsewhere and the rest of the world at large.

The next morning after breakfast Ambika and I took a long walk along Oceanic Drive, a scenic route that runs parallel to the coast to the tip of Point Cartwright. Skipped by many tourists who prefer to stay in Mooloolaba or Noosa, this was to be our introduction to the typical coastal 'Australian lifestyle' we'd read so much about.

The six-kilometre stretch of pathway hugs the coast, never losing sight of the golden sands and turquoise waters. We strolled past well-tended community parks, play areas and sandpits, skate rinks and open-air gyms, electric barbecues and log huts. As it was a weekday, it wasn't very crowded, but there were plenty of mums sitting under the shade of a mighty bunya tree or a giant paperbark while their children dressed in fluorescent swimwear and wide-brimmed hats played nearby. Now and then, cars pulled up and young men in wetsuits unstrapped their gleaming surfboards, polished smoother than a bowling ball, and headed to the beach for a surf. We passed joggers, couples, young and old out for walks as well as people sitting alone on the park benches lost in thought. On the horizon, we could make out the silhouettes of giant ocean liners steaming towards the Port of Brisbane while across the road, we gawked at row upon row of sprawling, whitewashed mansions with glass balustrades and expansive decks offering unobstructed views of the sea.

Our walk eventually led us to the Point Cartwright Lighthouse, standing proud and tall, offering stunning views of Mooloolaba, the Mooloolah River mouth, Mount Coolum to the north and Kawana Beach to the south. We spent the rest of the afternoon basking in the sun on the grassy knoll, watching sailboats cross the harbour, kids run freely in the park, and people enjoying meals at the posh waterfront cafés.

That evening, Ambika rustled up some chicken curry, much to the delight of Helen, who was craving for some authentic Indian cuisine. The term 'Indian' is an overused misnomer though as it often fails to represent the enormous variety of experiences the country has to offer. People often ask me to paint a picture of this ancient and mysterious land, a place steeped in tradition, overflowing with myriad spiritual beliefs and landscapes; from the snow-capped peaks of the majestic Himalayas in the north to the sun-kissed beaches, lush tropical forests and placid backwaters of the south.

'What does *real* Indian food taste like?'

'Does everyone in India practice Yoga?'

'Do all Indians pray to the Elephant God?'
'Do all people have an arranged marriage in India?'

It's hard for those who have never been to India to appreciate that it's a nation of a billion souls and a million contradictions; a giant juxtaposition where people worship a plethora of gods, engage in strange festivals and have customs that can seem downright bizarre to outsiders. The diverse and at times polarising religious beliefs sadly lead to a lack of a unified or coherent approach to many everyday problems. Yet, inexplicably, for the large part, despite all the oddities and dissimilarities, the billion hearts manage to beat as one.

Explaining the Indian ethos to an outsider is like trying to capture the singular meaning of a Picasso masterpiece. It's simply not possible. India is like a canvas that Picasso may well have painted. It conforms to his unique style of plasticising signs and symbols to the nth degree, forming abstract collages, and depicting geometric objects with the artistic inclination of a genius. Picasso once said, 'The several manners I have used in my art must not be considered as an evolution, or as steps towards an unknown ideal of painting … If the subjects I have wanted to express have suggested different ways of expression, I have never hesitated to adopt them.' India is something like that.

Although I have not visited every single corner of my homeland, I have backpacked around a fair bit, spending time in some of the most remote regions, including Arunachal Pradesh and Sikkim in the north-east; Kanyakumari at the south; and Andaman and Nicobar, a group of islands that lie closer to Thailand than mainland India. If there's one thing I've learnt it's that generalisations are futile. In India, every aspect of society changes every hundred kilometres – the cuisine, dress, language, culture, religion, political ideology, weather patterns, even people's physiology and skin tone.

India is a country that visitors either love or hate. If a foreigner steels himself upon arrival for the onslaught of culture shock and can refrain from being overwhelmed by the sheer scale of it all, he will be rewarded with rich and unforgettable experiences. As India's first prime minister, Jawaharlal Nehru, succinctly put it, 'India is a bundle of contradictions held together by strong but invisible threads.' Thousands of years of invasions, civilisations and migrations from all corners of the globe have created a potpourri of cultures that continue to blend and evolve to this day.

Take languages for example. Although India has twenty-two officially recognised languages, according to one census, there are 122 major languages and nearly 1600 other dialects spoken. For most individuals who migrated to bigger cities in search of better prospects, my parents included, it was not uncommon to speak three and at times, four distinct languages or dialects. By the time I got to talking age, I was already introduced to English (a default language courtesy of the British Raj), Hindi (the national language), Marathi (the state language), Kannada (the state language of my parents) and Konkani (our hometown dialect); by the time I was five, I was conversant in five different languages. Even Picasso would have been impressed.

Back in Helen's kitchen on the Sunshine Coast, Ambika had done a fine job of cooking a Mangalorean curry. (My parents hailed from Mangalore, a coastal city in the south-western state of Karnataka.) However, she was handicapped by the lack of spices and shredded coconut and served the dish with the disclaimer that it was far from a traditional version. It didn't matter: the golden-brown colour and the tingling aroma were sufficient to draw a grateful Helen and Ann to the table. Even Happy and Pugget seemed eager to share the meal but settled for the exclamations of appreciation from Helen as she savoured the curry with steaming basmati rice.

We were all getting along so well we decided to extend our stay. This would give us time to plan our onward journey and make the necessary bookings.

The following day we headed to Mooloolaba, the popular coastal suburb at the southern edge of the Sunshine Coast. The suburb offers one of the best beaches in Australia and scores of national and international events are held there every year. The esplanade facing Mooloolaba Beach houses the modern Sea Life aquarium as well as a range of souvenir shops, boutique clothing outlets, bookshops, galleries and restaurants.

At the visitor centre, we booked tickets on a whale-watching cruise that was due to depart that afternoon. While we waited for the boat to arrive, we had lunch at a waterfront Thai restaurant and couldn't help ogling at the million-dollar mansions, and beautiful yachts that zipped in and out of the harbour.

Whale-watching is a spectacular natural activity and should be on top of every traveller's bucket list. The seasonal migration occurs during the Antarctic winter when the warm-blooded mammals swim north along Australia's coastlines (on either side of the continent) to escape the frigid winter waters and breed. The pattern reverses at the start of the southern spring when the gentle giants return to their remote polar haven. Migration usually begins with the humpbacks who are then followed by the southern rights. Following the continental shelf, the majestic creatures travel up the coast as they playfully breach and blow their characteristic sprays of moist air and water. On average, more than 30,000 humpbacks (but only 3000 southern rights) make the 5000-kilometre trip each year.

Our four-hour return cruise aboard the 65-foot, twin-deck *Whale One* took us about 20 miles out to sea, right in the middle of the migration route. There was a slight swell that day, remnants of a cold front that had crossed the coast overnight, and this caused quite a few upset stomachs among the hundred or so whale watchers onboard. Thankfully, the crew had obviously dealt with such occurrences before and were quick to assist with plenty of barf bags at the ready. Seasickness aside, watching these magnificent creatures at arm's length was one of the most memorable things we've ever done. The excitement was palpable as everyone scanned the horizon for a tell-tale blow or splash. It seemed that the whales sensed our excitement and would swim close by to show off their skills. We saw three or four whales breach, clearly belonging to the same pod. One of the larger ones seemed in an especially joyous mood. On one occasion it came extremely close to the boat's bow and slapped its tail so hard that the spray engulfed all of us on the foredeck and the upper deck.

The return trip back to the harbour was a lot more comfortable, and there was a contented silence across the deck with most of the passengers reminiscing about the experience of the past hour. As we disembarked at the Mooloolaba jetty, another group of tourists was lining up ready to board. By this stage, the swell was increasing out at sea and we noticed one efficient staff member deftly walk up the gangplank with a fresh supply of barf bags. It was business as usual on board the *Whale One*.

That evening, Helen surprised us with an impromptu barbecue with Allen, her boyfriend, and her sister, Ann. 'A bit of an Aussie welcome for you guys,' she said. It was a touching gesture and we were grateful but also slightly apprehensive, wondering if the cultural differences would be a hindrance. Our fears proved unfounded. Helen and Ann were great company, and Allen an amputee with a prosthetic leg, was a stereotypical Australian bloke with self-deprecating humour. Medium built, with a receding hairline and a toothy grin, he cut the figure of a time-hardened person. He was a knockabout mechanic who owned a garage in Noosa and regaled us with his classic Australian humour while Helen shared numerous tales of their wild misadventures.

The couple introduced us to one of the most iconic Australian traditions – firing up a barbecue. This unique Australian tradition didn't take off until the 1950s when *The Australian Women's Weekly* ran a story on how to build one made of brick. Then in the mid-1960s, gas barbecues arrived, popping up in parks all over the country. Within a few decades, the tradition had become an ingrained part of the nation's psyche. Today, countless community events, weekend gatherings, election polling stations and even hardware stores are incomplete without a customary 'sausage sizzle' on a barbecue. Most Australian family homes have one neatly tucked in the corner of the backyard: some even have a secondary portable unit in the garden shed. The cooking method is straightforward, as Allen explained.

'You get a selection of sausages, some classic Australian steaks, some chicken tenders and lamb chops, marinate the raw meat and let it rest. Meanwhile, you get the fire going in the barbecue, chop a few onions and tenderise them, chuck in a few veggies, get it out of the way, and finally toss the meat on, all the time controlling the temperature, turning the food on the grill every once in a while. That's all there is to it, really.' This was one social skill that we were keen to pick up as soon as we were settled.

'So, why did you guys migrate to Australia?', Allen asked me casually whilst deftly turned the sausages over the sizzling grill. It was not the first time someone had posed this question to us, including our parents, and there was no straightforward answer. 'We migrated to Australia for the same reason we are undertaking this road trip ...', I replied, ' ... it's because we love travelling and exploring new places. Although giving up everything we had and moving to this country was not an easy decision, I reckoned it was worth the gamble, considering the abundance of opportunity that Australia presented, not just for us, but also for our kids, when they come along'. I cast a loving glance at Ambika whilst as I said this, because although I was speaking for both of us, deep down inside I knew that Ambika's primary reason to move was because of me. She had given up a whole lot more than I had in the process; I was a drifter ever since I had started sailing, and apart from my immediate family, I did not have much to consider when deciding to move. Ambika on the other hand had to give up her permanent job, put her career on hold, and bid adieu to her family and friends. And she did all of this with no reservations, only for me. I felt a deep sense of gratitude towards my beloved for having trusted me implicitly, and for having agreed to migrate to Australia only because she wanted to be with me. Yes, she was a special girl, and I was quite a lucky guy indeed.

As the night drew on and the wine bottles became lighter, Ann, ever the responsible one, retired, leaving the four of us to continue chatting. Helen told us she and Allen had recently chartered a houseboat for a couple of days. One evening, having decided to come ashore for dinner, they anchored the houseboat in the lee of an island and motored ashore in their tender. Halfway through dinner at a waterfront restaurant, Helen's sixth sense flickered and she told Allen she wanted to check on the houseboat. Allen, a few drinks down by then, was in a state of bliss and told her to rest her fears. When she got to the water's edge, she was horrified to see it was nowhere to be seen. She scanned the horizon and saw a faint light bobbing in the distance. She raced back into the restaurant, dragged Allen by the arm and rushed out – without even stopping to pay the bill. They were in their small tender in no time and sped off to catch the houseboat before it ran aground or drifted out to sea. They finally managed to catch up with the vessel, steer it to safety and re-anchor it.

One look at the forecastle revealed that Allen, in his haste to get to the restaurant, had failed to lay out the anchor properly. He was on his best behaviour for the rest of the trip after that.

One of the other stories that had us in splits was the naming of Helen's second pup. When Pugget was born, Helen asked Allen one evening what he thought would be a good name for the little mutt. Allen, who had already downed a few beers by then, was as interested in naming a pup as he was in figuring out the mysteries of the universe. He cheekily blurted out, 'I don't know … F@*!K it, Pug … itt!' And just like that, the little mutt got christened Pugget.

We shall always remember that particular night at Helen's as one of the most unexpected yet intensely warm gestures by any Airbnb host yet.

The next day, we returned to Mooloolaba to check out the Sea Life aquarium, rated as one of the Sunshine Coast's best attractions. The aquarium boasts a vast array of sea creatures, from dainty seahorses to dazzling starfish, acrobatic seals to giant barramundi. There's a multitude of themed sections from cavernous ocean tunnels to whispering billabongs, psychedelic jellyfish colonies and a section featuring sea creatures from the Great Barrier Reef. The most daring activity on offer however is the opportunity to swim with sharks.

I was a sailor, but that did not make me any less fearful of sharks, one of the most fearsome species on earth. I was, however, looking forward to the experience and took comfort in the trainer's words that these particular animals were used to being around people and were quite safe. Ambika, however, had never even been snorkelling before and here I was asking her to start learning in a shark-infested tank! I thought she might refuse, but she was totally unfazed. Ambika was proving to be a compatible partner, who was free spirited and shared my sense of adventure. The trainers did a fantastic job teaching us the basics, and one of them was alongside Ambika the entire time.

The experience of swimming with the multi-coloured fish alone was incredible. There was a moment when Tsunami, the resident giant ray, passed right below me, and I lightly brushed against his fan-like body more in awe than with curiosity. The ultimate thrill, however, was coming eye to eye with the sharks. Every time one of these imposing creatures swam past I could see its gills flutter with each breath and feel the cold, lifeless eyes staring right at me. This was one of the most daring things Ambika and I have ever done, and the feeling of exhilaration stayed with us for a long time afterwards.

After our adventure at the Sea Life aquarium, we visited the local markets in Mooloolaba and then, out of curiosity, checked out one of the many local caravan parks. Ambika and I came from a world where caravanning, fishing and four-wheel driving were alien concepts, the province of the wealthy upper class. In Australia, though, these activities were almost second nature, with parents getting their children involved from a very early age. There was a great variety of caravans and campervans on show at this particular park – tent trailers; pop-tops, pop-outs; camper trailers and motorhomes.

It'd be a while until we mustered the courage to embark on a caravanning trip ourselves, but I was itching to see the insides of one of these mobile homes nonetheless. Before Ambika could shoot down the idea, I approached an elderly couple who were sitting in fold-out chairs outside their caravan in the shade of the awning. The silver-haired man was busy working on a crossword while the lady, whom I presumed was his wife, read the newspaper. I asked the couple politely if they wouldn't mind us intruding on their private space. The woman immediately got defensive, but the elderly gentleman appeared bemused, sensing Ambika's reluctance. (She was crouching behind me, wishing for the earth to swallow her entirely.)

'If you're selling religion, we're not buying!' she cried defensively.

'Not at all,' I said hastily, 'we're new to this country and just wanted to learn about the Australian lifestyle. We were wondering if you could tell us a little bit about caravanning as we've never done it.'

The change in the woman's demeanour was instantaneous. She dropped her guard, put down her newspaper and flashed us a broad smile. 'Oh, of course, my name's Chrissy. My husband Jim and I'd be happy to show you around and give you some tips.' Jim jumped out of his chair as if this was the most exciting thing that had happened all day. It probably was. Meanwhile, Ambika came out of hiding from behind my back, flashing her beautiful smile as if indicating that this was her idea all along. It turned out the couple had recently retired and had used some of their life savings to take an extended trip around Australia, starting their adventure in their hometown of Adelaide in South Australia. I was to later learn that there's a significant number of retiree-couples like Jim and Chrissy – affectionately known as 'grey nomads' – travelling the country at any one time. Jim showed me his copy of the *Explore Australia by Caravan and Motorhome*, a comprehensive book covering almost all of the routes around Australia which included a handy section on safety tips and practical advice for first-timers. Chrissy then invited us to have a look inside. We were impressed. Although a mid-range caravan, the compact interior was tastefully decorated and had all the mod-cons you could hope for. We thanked the couple for indulging us, to which they responded with a characteristically unassuming 'No worries', wishing us safe onward travels.

We ended up staying at Helen's villa for nearly a week, but eventually, we felt the gentle tug of the open road. We were sad to leave. In no time at all, we had developed a warm friendship with these total strangers. During the last two days of our stay, Helen and Allen went to Noosa, entrusting us with the care of the house and her pet dogs. We gladly accepted but couldn't help wondering how she came to be so trusting of people she'd only just met.

'Jason, if someone wanted to take something from my house, he probably needs it more than me,' she told us. What a remarkable attitude! It was hard to part with the dogs as well. Although I've never had a dog of my own, I've always loved being around them. However, this was the first time I was responsible for minding two dogs, and I loved every moment of it. We were supposed to feed them twice a day, and at mealtimes they would come bounding towards me, looking up at me with mellow coal-black eyes, their soft, curious noses twitching with anticipation. On the last evening of our stay, we took them for a long walk with us, knowing that we probably would never see them again.

After a big round of hugs and goodbyes, Ann kindly dropped us at the train station in Maroochydore, where we would board the *Spirit of Queensland* for our first long-distance rail journey. Our next destination was Mackay.

CHAPTER 8

Romancing the Railways

The journey has its own lyrics. A duet of balanced motion, the rails and wheels in tune – Richard L. Ratliff

There's no point taking a train journey in Australia if you're pressed for time or on a strict budget. Train trips typically take far longer and are more expensive when compared to relatively cheap air travel. Most tourists coming to Australia would understandably prefer to visit more places rather than spend all their time leisurely moving from one destination to another in a locomotive.

I have a different view, however, and am enamoured by the concept of rail journeys. Irrespective of where I go, I find that train travel offers a unique perspective, laying bare the heart of a region – without filters or glamour. For me, long-distance train journeys evoke a sense of romance and nostalgia that can transcend time and place. Think of the buzz of activity on the platform as the departure time draws near; the poignant goodbyes; the last-minute adjustments; the train master's final whistle; the waving of the green flag; the deliberate *chug-chug* of the wheels as the train springs to life; the last glimpse of familiar scenes being left behind; and the *clackity-clack* of wheels as the train gains momentum. The childlike pleasure of placing your forehead against the window and watching the unfolding scenery – in slow motion or a rapid blur – never seems to lose its magic. Train travel presents life 'in limbo' like no other mode of transport.

Back home in India, when we were growing up - and this was way before the advent of low-cost airlines - rail travel was an essential part of most of our long-distance journeys. Irrespective of the destination or the sector travelled, every journey had its own distinct flair - the specific class of train servicing the route, the sights and sounds of the local townships, the heady aroma of local delicacies intermingled with the characteristic scent of the region, the vistas which ranged from barren land to verdant rainforests, and the topography of the land which varied from flat coastal plains to steep mountain ranges. However, the dominant feature of all the rail journeys I have had in India - and the one I found most striking - was the sheer mass of people and the variety of experiences one encountered - from towering turbans to Gandhi caps, from traditional sarees to floral skirts, from saffron-robed monks to ash-smeared sadhus, from chic city dwellers to rural country folk - it was impossible, even as a local traveller, to be unmoved by the spectacle of a classic Indian railroad journey.

We thus excitedly boarded the *Spirit of Queensland* at Nambour on the Sunshine Coast headed for Mackay, an overnight journey which would cover roughly 850 kilometres, eager to sample a flavour of Australian rail travel. Connecting Brisbane to Cairns, the *Spirit of Queensland* offers a modern rail travel experience and access to some spectacular holiday destinations along the way – the Great Barrier Reef, the Whitsundays, Townsville and Cairns, to name just a few.

As we were on a budget, we opted for economy class tickets, but at nearly $400, they weren't the cheapest, either. The facilities onboard, however, were excellent and would put most airline business class travel to shame. The seats in our compartment had soft leather upholstery, plenty of legroom, and nine-inch entertainment screens loaded with an excellent selection of movies and documentaries. The train also had a separate diner carriage with a bar offering la carte menus as well as light refreshments, cold beers and a selection of fine wines. Most compartments had bathrooms with shower facilities.

Sitting in the comforts of the modern carriage, I reflected upon the history of Australian railways and the hardships faced at the dawn of the rail era. The vast Australian rail network bears testimony to those pioneers and early settlers who dared venture into unknown territory in the name of exploration, laying down the tracks with their bare hands, one laborious mile after another. The famous 'Ghan' line, for example, which runs north-south linking Adelaide with Darwin, is rightly regarded as one of the world's great rail journeys. The journey takes passengers through one of the last untamed, pristine and utterly astonishing landscapes in the world.

The name supposedly honours the Afghan camel drivers who arrived in Australia in the late nineteenth century with animals imported from India. Starting in Adelaide, the train takes you north across vast plains, chugging under the watchful shadows of the Flinders Ranges, before passing through Alice Springs in the 'red centre' of the country; the world's iconic destination that represents total isolation, Coober Pedy, famous for its opals and searing heat; and Tennant Creek, a centre of gold mining.

Attractions along the Ghan's route aside, one of the simplest yet most primal pleasures of this train trip is the opportunity to behold the countless, twinkling heavenly bodies in an untainted inky black night sky or witness captivating sunrises and sunsets on the distant horizon against the backdrop of the vast Australian Outback.

Another epic Australian route, this one running east-west from Sydney to Perth, is the equally famous 'Indian Pacific'. Covering some 4300 kilometres, the train crosses the hot and dusty Nullarbor Plain, taking three leisurely days to complete the journey. This section of the trip lays claim to having the longest stretch of pencil-straight track in the world – 478 kilometres – surreally planted in one of the flattest places on earth. . So demanding was the terrain across the Nullarbor, that it was described as 'a hideous anomaly, a blot on the face of Nature, the sort of place one gets into in bad dreams' by novelist and travel writer, Henry Kingsley.

Arguably the first significant work of a federated Australia, the line was originally called the 'Trans-Australian Railway' and was intended to link Port Augusta in South Australia with Kalgoorlie in Western Australia.

Prior to the Federation in 1901, the eastern Australian colonies had laid a condition on the western provinces: if they were to be a part of the joint federation and enjoy the privileges of the Commonwealth, a railway link was needed. This was no high-handed, whimsical demand as a result of power struggles between the colonies. The reason was more practical and had to do with the survival of Australia as a new nation. In those days, the only link between east and west was a rough coastal sea voyage. Commerce and trade were restricted and, if the proposed federation was to ever defend Australia's southern and western shores, moving troops and supplies would be extremely difficult without an alternate route.

Work on the railway began in earnest in 1912, with tracks built simultaneously in both directions, east from Port Augusta and west from Kalgoorlie. It took five years to finish the 1693-kilometre job.

It wasn't until 1969 that a standard gauge rail network was extended east from Port Augusta to Sydney, and west of Kalgoorlie to Perth, making it the 'Indian Pacific' as it is known today. The line now runs on an unbroken track from the Pacific Ocean all the way across the continent to the Indian Ocean.

Back aboard the *Spirit of Queensland*, our very own 'real time' train journey was unfolding marvellously. As our trip began at night, I cracked open a can of beer and settled in to watch a film. Ambika chose the perfect title *Tracks*, an adaptation of the famous memoir by Robyn Davidson chronicling her incredible nine-month camel trek across the harsh Australian desert.

Aged eighteen and dissatisfied with the direction life was taking her, Robyn decided to move from Sydney to Alice Springs. There, she trained camels and learnt how to survive for two years before embarking on an odyssey which would forever change her life. In 1977, with her dog and four camels, she travelled west from Alice Springs across 2700 kilometres of harsh and merciless desert to the Indian Ocean. Her 273-day journey took her through some of the harshest and most desolate terrain in the world, across endless deserts and via remote Indigenous settlements and outposts.

Ambika and I were fascinated and yet found it hard to imagine why someone would undertake such a hazardous solo voyage. In her travel memoir, Davidson wrote that it was difficult to explain, but if there was any moral to her story, it was that 'one can be awake to the demand for obedience that seems natural, simply because it is familiar'. She especially loved 'the big, big spaces and possibilities' that 'are metaphors for other things'. Her central message – that we can all push the boundaries, disobey the rules and experiment with life – resonated strongly with us.

As dawn broke, Ambika and I were greeted with our first glimpse of tropical North Queensland, a countryside lush with many shades of green as far as the eye could see. Tall eucalypts and forest oaks lined the train tracks, providing glimpses of the rugged mountains of the Great Dividing Range to our left, and the forested plains that hemmed the coastline to our right. Farms and vast acreages, with their borders fenced-in into neat rectangle blocks, lay interspaced between wild forested land.

Every so often, kangaroos and wallabies would leap from the bushland, startled by the sound of the train. Occasionally, we'd pass a country town comprising a few low-set houses tightly bunched together, a church with its tall dominating spire at the centre. On the town's outskirts, there'd be the ubiquitous pub, a wooden signboard swaying gently in the breeze, inviting the country folk in for a beer and a round of gossip after a long day in the fields.

Everywhere we looked were endless rows of sugar cane. Over two metres tall, the crop was just a few months away from the end-of-year harvest. The history of sugar cane farming in Australia dates back to 1788 when the First Fleet arrived at Botany Bay, but the industry took off in the mid-1800s when the first viable plantations were established near Brisbane. Today, the Australian sugar cane industry is one of the world's most efficient and innovative and the country ranks as one of the top raw sugar exporters in the world.

Ironically, the foundation of the industry is inexorably linked to the settlement of non-whites at a time when much of Australia was vehemently opposed to non-white migration. Apart from South Sea Islanders – who were indentured labourers brought into the country in a practice known as 'Blackbirding', countless Italians migrated to escape poverty and strife in their own country, while Sikh migrants from India – many of whom were regimental sepoys who followed the British army officers across Asia for postings – soon realised there were tremendous opportunities in Australia and decided to stay and seek their fortunes. The first Italians and Sikhs arrived in the late 1830s at a time when the inflow of convicts was declining. The shortage of manual labour had led to increasing demand, and the migrants, many of whom came from a traditional agrarian background, were well suited to work as farm labourers and shepherds.

Nowadays, Australia's Sikh farming community is considered one of the most culturally unique and forward-thinking anywhere in the world. Take for example Woolgoolga, a little seaside town with a population of around 5000 some 550 kilometres north of Sydney on the mid-north coast of New South Wales. Originally founded in a typically British style, visitors today would be forgiven for mistaking it as a rural town in India's Punjab region! Sikhs began moving here from north Queensland shortly after World War II ended. Once better known for bananas and sugar cane, the industrious newcomers transformed the region and planted blueberries, developing them into a multi-million-dollar industry. The Sikh blueberry co-operative has been a huge success and the broader Coffs Harbour region now accounts for around 80 per cent of Australia's total production. It exports its product to all corners of the world – even to India!

We were learning a lot about the history of Australian agriculture. But it was mid-morning by now and our train had just arrived at Mackay, the next stop in our epic journey of discovery.

CHAPTER 9

Heart of the Reef

The best experiences can't be forced, and they come when you least expect it. You don't find misadventure, it finds you – S.A. Tawks, Misadventurous

The town of Mackay was established along the banks of the Pioneer River, about 1000 kilometres north of Brisbane, in the 1860s. Within a decade, it had become the region's 'sugar capital', with some sixteen mills springing up and almost 5000 acres of land under cultivation. In the 1970s, however, coal mining took over from sugar cane and these days, mining is the main employer of the town's approximately 80,000 people. The mining industry is at the centre of much debated climate-change discussion and as such does not enhance Mackay's reputation with international tourists. While the debate goes on, it is no doubt that coal exports add significantly to the federal coffers and play a vital role in Australia's economic success.

We were in Mackay for mainly personal reasons – to visit an acquaintance whom I had got to know on a previous sailing job. When we arrived, Glenn Saldanha, a friend of my ex-boss, was working, and had asked one of his colleagues to pick us up from the train station. We caught up with Glenn later in the afternoon over lunch, and he offered to take us home to meet his family and stay overnight. Glenn is built big but has the persona of a gentle giant. With a commanding voice and a steady gaze, he's a 'people person' – someone who can talk at length on seemingly any topic under the sun. He's also well-connected both in Australia and in India, and we had fun comparing notes on people we knew from our seafaring days. Glenn's wife Gizelle, whom we met later that night, has an air of gentleness and a soft lilting voice and a quiet demeanour.

The couple migrated to Australia in 2000 with their two children, now in their teens. Glenn works as a coastal marine pilot on the Great Barrier Reef, guiding ships through the sensitive eco-system. A ship's captain and crew seldom have the luxury of taking in the sights when transiting the constricted waterway; they're more worried about navigating the treacherous waters without getting into trouble. The Great Barrier Reef is a twisted labyrinth of jagged reefs – some lying less than 600 metres from the shipping channel. To add to this, mariners are faced with complex tidal flows, unpredictable weather conditions, shallow waters and tropical rain squalls. Marine accidents, mercifully, are rare, and this is in large part due to the strict pilotage regime implemented by the Australian government.

Glenn pilots ships through the narrow confines of the Hydrographer's Passage deep-water shipping channel. Some of the vessels that use the channel are over 250 metres long and weigh over 200,000 tons fully laden. The narrow passage, which is about 115 nautical miles from the mainland, offers the shortest and most economical route for vessels heading for the bulk loading ports of Hay Point, Dalrymple Bay and Mackay. Approximately 80 nautical miles in length, the channel is well marked but experiences strong tidal streams. At its narrowest point at the seaward entrance between White Tip Reef and Bonds Reef, it's only 1.5 nautical miles wide. Once past this entry point, ships make a series of significant alterations in quick succession, avoiding the shallow waters and low-lying reefs that threaten to rip the guts out of any boat deviating from its course.

An average day sees Glenn boarding a helicopter at Mackay before flying out to Blossom Bank to rendezvous with the incoming ship. He's then transferred aboard the moving vessel in almost a James Bond fashion! Once safely on the bridge of the vessel, he discusses the passage plan with the master and his team and then expertly guides the ship through the reef system. Conditions are seldom ideal, but Glenn makes these trips day or night, rain or shine, the helicopter often conducting pilot transfers on ships that roll in the ocean swell.

Although we'd planned to stay and explore Mackay, Glenn suggested we'd have better options for sightseeing in the Whitsundays and recommended we visit Airlie Beach, gateway to the Reef, around 120 kilometres north of Mackay.

After lunch, he took me around town while he ran some errands. This gave me the chance to meet some of his friends and get a feel for living in a small, tight-knit community. One couple we met worked at the local hospital. Their multi-level home offered a stupendous view of the surrounding suburbs and had an indoor pool, hand-carved furniture, plush Persian rugs and expensive murals and paintings. As we left, Glenn pointed to another house, smaller in size and grandeur which belonged to a tradesman (or 'tradie' as they were known in Australia) – a plumber who owned a local business. It was clear Australia was a country that offered plenty of opportunities, irrespective of your profession. More importantly, there seemed to be no class distinction; everyone could enjoy the same benefits and equal opportunities – having a 'fair go', as Australians like to call it.

We spent the night at Glenn's house, an immaculately maintained modern, low-set, four-bedroom, two-bathroom bungalow with a raised patio deck and small, well-tended backyard. At the dinner table, Ambika and I shared our backpacking stories and our rough itinerary. We also mentioned our apprehension about going from carefree vagabonds to domesticated migrants in a new country.

'It's a funny business, this migration and settling-down process, and it gets more challenging if you migrate later in life,' Glenn said. 'You move overseas lured by the lifestyle, by the ability to do so many leisure activities and by the fact that you have some of the most beautiful places in the world in your very own backyard. Yet most of us from the Indian subcontinent are more focused on ensuring the financial stability of the family. This stems from our age-old habit of saving for a rainy day, a habit so ingrained in our psyche we sometimes postpone our own personal gratification and forget to enjoy the rewards we set out to achieve in the first place.'

Gizelle echoed Glenn's sentiments. 'We migrated quite late in our lives and our goal was always to ensure that our kids would get the best education and opportunities that we never had. It was difficult – the separation from family, colleagues and friends was hard to deal with, especially for our kids, whom we uprooted from school and from friends they grew up with. But that's all in the past now. We've established ourselves in this community, have made some great friends and are happy for our children who are doing well.'

Glenn said the degree of longing for India increased in proportion to age at the time of migration. He still missed traditional Indian food, his childhood friends, work colleagues whom he knew for decades and his extended family, though not necessarily in that order.

'With the benefit of hindsight,' I asked, 'would you reconsider your decision to migrate if offered a second chance?'

'Not at all,' they replied without hesitation. 'The only regret we have is that we didn't migrate earlier!'

Feeling enthused and motivated, we went to bed, hoping that we too would eventually make our mark in this remarkable land that rewarded those who dared to dream.

Next morning, Gizelle dropped us at the bus stop. We'd said our goodbyes to Glenn the night before as he had an early start and had left home in the pre-dawn hours to pilot the next inbound ship into the Hydrographer's Passage.

Our first Australian bus trip would take us to Airlie Beach, about two hours north of Mackay. Peter, our driver, turned out to be full of amusing stories and historical anecdotes. Apart from providing a running commentary on passing landmarks and Australian history in general, he'd regularly rouse the backpackers snoring away at the rear of the bus.

We settled into the first row so we'd have a good view of the passing countryside. The Bruce Highway was slick with tropical rain from the previous night, and the asphalt gleamed like the back of a humpback whale. The lush foliage reached the edge of the modern highway, and the tall coconut trees and the native gum trees gave the region a laid-back tropical feel.

We soon passed the town of The Leap, population 673. Outside the town's hotel, we noticed a statue of a woman running with a baby tucked under her arm.

'That's Kohawa,' our bus driver Peter said. 'She's a part of the local folklore, although her story is tragic. Back in 1887, clashes between the newly arrived white settlers and the Indigenous people were occurring every day. The white man's need for land meant that the Indigenous people were pushed further away from the new settlements. Their plight was compounded by the fact that they placed little value on the goods that were offered to them in return. Tired of the daily skirmishes, the local white farmers approached the local police, asking for them to intervene and put a stop to the hostilities. The cops decided to catch a group of Indigenous people and jail them. A chase ensued and a young Aboriginal lady named Kohawa who had just been blessed with a baby got caught in the mêlée. She was cornered on the edge of a cliff atop one of the surrounding mountains. Seeing no escape, she leapt from the cliff's edge with her baby tucked under her arm.'

We were soon to learn that Australia's Indigenous people had been the traditional owners of the country for tens of thousands of years before the first white man arrived, but since then they'd suffered countless atrocities and hardships.

'The only consolation in all of this,' Pete added, 'was the fact that the baby miraculously survived and was later adopted by one of the settler families, baptised and eventually bore kids of her own.'

Thanks to Peter's engaging stories and the scenic drive, we reached the Airlie Beach turn-off before we knew it. The road branched from the Bruce Highway at Proserpine, a picturesque farming town named by the explorer George Dalrymple after Persephone the Greek goddess of fertility in recognition of the region's fertile qualities. Established in the 1890s, the town's economic mainstay used to be cattle grazing and sugar. Today, the borough caters to the endless stream of tourists while managing to still retain its colonial charm.

Airlie Beach is a compact resort town, crammed with colourful tour guide centres, inviting cocktail bars, seaside cafés, expensive-looking resorts and quirky souvenir and retail shops. The coast curves and twists at the water's edge, creating natural bays and small pockets of beachfront which offer idyllic getaways for holidaymakers. Out on the celestial blue waters, dozens of yachts bobbed gently in the marinas. The town has a distinct party vibe – not the thumping, crazy-beat, late-night party kind – but rather an all-inclusive, subdued, 'life-is-beautiful' vibe that celebrates life in the tropics.

'Here we are, folks,' Peter said. 'Welcome to the "Heart of the Reef" terminal. Back in the day, we'd just called it a bus stop, but clearly, times have moved on. Now it's all about making the place glamorous in the glossy travel magazines and brochures.'

The bus terminal was named after one of the most iconic reefs in the Whitsundays, a stunning composition of coral in the shape of a heart. Located in Hardy Reef, Heart Reef is best experienced from the air in a helicopter or seaplane. Needless to say, it's been the site of many proposals and declarations of love over the years.

Airlie Beach offers unparalleled access to the Great Barrier Reef and the Whitsundays, a group of seventy-four islands that lie off the coast and form part of the Reef. With appealing names like Hamilton, Hayman and Daydream, these islands serve as ideal stepping stones to the pristine wonderland, the Reef. The islands cater to all budgets – from bespoke seven-star accommodation with private charter seaplanes, to bush walks through virgin forests. You can hire sailboats to visit the nearby reefs, snorkel and scuba dive, and even spend a night in the middle of the Reef, suspended on a floating ramp. With its pristine beaches, turquoise waters and lush tropical forests right to the water's edge, Airlie Beach and Shute Harbour are undoubtedly two of the most idyllic spots in Australia.

We thanked Peter for an informative bus trip. As a parting shot, he told us a joke.

'My mate Ricky decides to go back home to Melbourne, so he calls Qantas to book his flight. The operator asks him, "How many people are flying with you?"

'Ricky replies, "Strewth, mate, how would I know? It's your plane!"'

With that, Peter bade us a great holiday and waved us goodbye.

CHAPTER 10

Flight of Fancy

Roam abroad in the world, and take thy fill of its enjoyments before the day shall come when thou must quit it for good – Saadi

We'd booked a two-bedroom Airbnb unit on an elevated foothill of the Conway National Park about 1.5 kilometres from the bus terminal. I had assumed that we could easily manage that distance on foot with our backpacks and wheelie bag. What I hadn't counted on was the uphill climb in the blazing heat and humidity at nearly 90 per cent! Weighed down by our bags and struggling, Airlie Beach suddenly didn't feel like a beach paradise at all. The most disconcerting part was Ambika's angry glare that threatened to melt me into a puddle of nothingness on the hot asphalt. I shrank down under my backpack like a hermit crab retreating into his shell, eyes on the road, pretending to be unfazed.

Ambika was adventurous and, in the short time I had known her, had proved to be a resourceful and resilient traveller, taking almost everything in her stride. However, there were some 'no-go' zones when it came to likes/dislikes and personal comfort, and I had just crossed a line. To add to our misery, we hadn't had a decent meal since morning, and we were lugging 15-kilogram backpacks and a wheelie bag. I know Ambika loves me unreservedly, but I got the feeling on this occasion I pushed things a little bit too far. I have since learnt that in times like this, men must remain silent.

Help soon arrived from an unexpected quarter. As we were soldiering up the hill – one of us fuming and the other playing it cool – a car slowed down and pulled over to the side of the road, and a young woman got out.

'Hey guys, my name's Emily,' she said with a friendly smile. 'Looks like you could use a lift on a hot day like this.' She pointed to her little Holden Barina. The car had seen better days, but we didn't care – at that moment it felt as if it was the most beautiful automobile we'd ever seen, and we wasted no time leaping inside. We were in for another surprise as a chubby little infant lay in a baby capsule in the back seat. Baby Tristan floored us with his angelic, toothless smile and his constant cooing – blissfully unaware of the singular act of charity his mum had just displayed. It was a short five-minute drive to our destination, which gave us time enough to learn that Emily was a nurse at the local hospital but was currently on maternity leave.

'Weren't you apprehensive when you offered us a ride?' Ambika asked her.

'We're lucky to live in a region spared from the vagaries of the outside world,' Emily replied. 'We get a lot of visitors and most of them are well-behaved. Apart from the stunning countryside, they come here to experience our simple, relaxed lifestyle. The biggest blessing for us in this small community is the fact that we still trust people and believe in the inherent goodness of mankind. Will Tristan be equally lucky when he grows up? I really hope so.' She nodded towards her baby boy who was busy clutching Ambika's pinkie finger and kicking his pudgy feet with excitement.

Emily left us at our apartment block which was on the top of the ridge. Although I did not doubt that it offered the best views in town, I shuddered to think I'd considered walking all the way here from the bus stop. Thanks to Emily's act of charity, peace prevailed in paradise. We hugged her and thanked her profusely. Ambika was grateful for the timely help while I was grateful Emily had got me off the hook.

Mandy, our Airbnb host, was a stewardess on one of the big charter boats that cruised around the Whitsunday Islands. She told us she'd be working for the duration of our stay and had made arrangements for us to collect the keys and check ourselves in. For the next three days, we had the whole place to ourselves.

With views across the glorious Airlie Bay on one side and the green canopy of the Conway National Park on the other, the apartment truly was spectacular.

That evening we walked into town to get our bearings, which took all of one hour, by which time we had been up and down the main street twice. Proserpine's Shute Harbour Road slices through the heart of the town and meanders along the coast. It ends abruptly at Shute Harbour, about 11 kilometres further down the track from Airlie Beach.

Despite its name, Airlie Beach has mostly small crescent-shaped alcoves – not great for crowds of tourists. To make up for this, it has a fantastic man-made lagoon strategically located in the centre of town, overlooking the picturesque Airlie Bay. Over 200 metres long and 50 metres wide, the lagoon has an arched footbridge, swaying palm trees and well-manicured lawns. There are stretches of artificial sandy beach and scores of shaded rest areas, picnic tables, garden benches and community barbecues. The place celebrates the Australian beachside lifestyle, and was filled with holiday-makers but far from crowded. Bikini-clad women and men in colourful boardshorts lay sprawled on beach towels at the water's edge, their tanned bodies gleaming in the evening sunlight. Little children made the best of the kiddie pool section while their parents watched on. Some families had set up beach chairs and camp tables for an evening picnic and the aromas of grilled food wafted from the barbecues to all the corners of the park.

To celebrate our arrival in this little pocket of paradise, we splurged on a bottle of red wine. For dinner, we stuck to our trusted and economical meal option – the humble foot-long Subway sandwich. At just $10, this was our go-to meal while on the road. We preferred splurging on experiences and balancing the expenses by taming our appetites and eating cheaply. Luckily, both of us detested junk food (however, we did have our weak moments during the trip) and Subway sandwiches were a reasonably healthy meal we could always bank on.

The setting for our romantic dinner was Mandy's verandah with its commanding view of the town. Sitting under the soft moonlight, we could hear the gentle lapping of the waters as the waves caressed the foreshore. The distant sounds of the sea co-mingled with the earthy beats emanating from the forest nearby: the occasional rustling of the branches on the paperbark and pandanus trees, the persistent sound of crickets and the intermittent croaking of frogs. That evening ranks as one of the most magical, intimate and romantic moments of our entire trip.

The next morning, we awoke energised and, after our dose of morning coffee and a sumptuous home-cooked breakfast, we took a short hike in the Conway National Park. Later, we sauntered into town as I was keen to fix my SLR camera which hadn't worked since our whale-watching excursion at Mooloolaba.

Our search led us to the local fish and tackle shop at the edge of the town. The shop catered to casual day-trippers fishing off the jetty edge as well as to deep-sea charters who specialised in spearfishing and big game fishing. This was our first ever visit to a fish and tackle shop, so we were in awe at all the items on display. Back in India, fishing is not a sport, at least not for the general populace. In Australia, however, it is almost a religion; a rite of passage for kids who are exposed to it from a young age – be it fishing off the jetty with a fishing rod or an outing in a 'tinnie' with mum and dad. Indeed, whenever I mentioned to locals that I'd never been fishing, they looked at me wide-eyed as if I'd committed sacrilege.

Geoff, the owner of the shop, greeted us with a broad smile. With his sun-wizened features, white beard, striking blue Hawaiian shirt and off-white cotton shorts, he looked every bit the toughened sailor. He and his team repaired fishing equipment in the store, so he was well equipped and immediately went out to the rear to grab the appropriate tools for my camera. As we were the only customers, we struck up a conversation and told him a bit about our backpacking trip. An avid motorcyclist, Geoff had a custom-built Harley-Davidson and he told us about his most recent solo road trip from the coastal town of Rockhampton to the remote township of Longreach in central Queensland. The land he travelled through was ancient and held secrets and mysteries dating back millions of years.

Geoff told us of the long, desolate roads with not a single passing vehicle for hours at end, and the difficult living conditions faced by the rural communities. He showed us photographs of ramshackle taverns, single-pump, roofless petrol stations which offered no shade, and bleached skulls of cattle perched on roadside fences – sharp reminders that the Australian outback was a merciless and demanding place.

One of the most striking images he showed us was of a mammoth road train – a giant beast of a truck, some examples of which could stretch for 60 metres from the front of the cab to the end of the last trailer and carry more than 200 tons of goods. The invention of the road train, as with most other inventions, came out of sheer necessity. The flat terrain of the continent, arrow-straight roads and the vast distances between destinations make Australia the perfect place for extremely long road vehicles.

Today, road trains transport livestock, fuel, mineral ores, and general freight and the cost savings play a significant part in the economic development of the remote regions. Geoff told us it's an experience watching one of these trucks come barrelling down the highway. 'The sheer volume of air it displaces as it whizzes past is enough to rattle even the sturdiest of 4WDs. I prudently chose to stop on the shoulder and get off my bike every time I saw one of these monsters coming over the horizon.'

I eventually managed to get my camera casing open but soon realised that it was as far as I was going to get. The sea salt had somehow found its way into the shutter mechanism and the camera was pretty much useless. Luckily, we had a secondary digital camera which we used for the remainder of the trip.

Later that day, after a light meal at the appropriately named diner and pub The Beaches, we took a plunge in the Airlie Lagoon then spent the rest of the afternoon basking in the sun and enjoying the views. We had however kept the best for last and on our final day at Airlie Beach, we were off for our very own 'millionaire experience'!

In a moment of extravagance, we'd booked a seaplane ride to Whitehaven Beach on the eastern side of Whitsunday Island. Consistently rated as one of the best in the world, the beach has about seven kilometres of powder-fine, brilliant white sand. It's 98 per cent pure silica and we'd read it feels like talcum powder under your feet. The sheltered waters are crystal clear and make for perfect swimming while the coastline is backed by dense tropical rainforests which cover the entire island.

The three-hour round trip put a dent in our budget, but we figured that some experiences were just worth it. Our Canadian-built de Havilland Beaver seaplane took us over Shute Harbour, the Molle group of islands, Whitsunday Passage, Whitsunday Island, and the magnificent swirling sands of Hill Inlet. We landed on the placid aquamarine waters of Whitehaven Beach, having shared our ride with another couple, Eric and Karina from Germany.

We hopped off gingerly into the foot-deep aquamarine water and waded to the shore where the flight skipper offered us a picnic hamper with sparkling wine and nibbles. We were then left to ourselves for a good hour on the beach to take a swim and relax. Although there were quite a few other tourists, most coming via boat on island-hopping tours, there was ample room for all and the beach did not feel crowded. Ambika and I managed to find a secluded spot and shared a few romantic moments in a picture-perfect landscape. The pure white sands were just as wonderful as we'd imagined.

As it generally transpires when you share private moments in close proximity with your fellow travellers, you develop a particular bond. So it was in our case, and by the time we headed back to Airlie Beach in the seaplane, we were chatting away with Eric and Karina who were on a whirlwind Australian tour in a campervan. We had never seen the inside of a campervan, and I asked them if we could have a look. They did one better and offered to drive us back to the bus terminal in the town centre.

Their campervan had the entire aft portion stripped off with just one seat which folded into a makeshift bed. The rear was filled with their possessions and provisions for the journey. It seemed like an exciting thing to do, but Ambika and I had reservations given we'd never driven anything bigger than a sedan. We always had pictured 'campervaners' to be fringe tourists who smoked weed and stayed on the outskirts of the town in shady, makeshift camps. This was until we learnt more about designated caravan parks and the myriad other facilities available to such travellers in Australia. Eric and Karina dropped us off in the town centre and, after saying their goodbyes, sped off to their next destination.

We had a six-hour wait for our bus which was due to leave at 8.30 p.m. that night. As we'd already checked out of Mandy's Airbnb apartment, we decided to settle into one of the gazebos which fronted the Airlie Lagoon. With a daypack as our pillow, a backpack as our footrest and a few seagulls and cockatoos for company, we whiled away the time reading and snoozing. The gentle sea breeze, the sound of the waves lazily lapping on the shore and the fresh memories of Whitehaven Beach soon put me to sleep. Ambika, on the other hand, used the time to sift through the photos and update our travel journal.

It doesn't take much to shed your inhibitions once you adapt to life on the road as a backpacker. In a single day, we had snoozed in a public place, walked barefoot into a shop and managed to take a semi-shower in a restroom, illegally of course. I sensed Ambika was a bit out of her comfort zone, but she played along and followed my lead like the good sport she was. By the time we wandered over to the bus terminal, we were well-fed, well-rested and eager to reach our next destination – Cairns.

CHAPTER 11
Ancient Land and Old Culture

Australian history does not read like history, but like the most beautiful lies – Mark Twain, Following the Equator

Australia is a harsh continent, with vast parts covered by unforgiving terrain and ruled by extreme weather. Much of the land remains unexplored, with areas larger than some countries depicted on maps simply as 'unsurveyed terrain' – flat, featureless zones whose faint dotted lines fail to convey the ever-present dangers and unpredictable conditions. Many communities are represented by just a tiny dot. Cape York in Far North Queensland, known as 'The Tip' by locals, is one such place.

The Bruce Highway, which runs from Brisbane up the Queensland coast for nearly 1700 kilometres, ends at Cairns, Australia's fourth most popular destination after Sydney, Melbourne and Brisbane. Loved by backpackers, adventure junkies and anyone looking for a bona fide tropical experience, Cairns offers a variety of activities in and around the world-famous Great Barrier Reef and pulsates with its unique holiday beat.

For most, Cairns marks the final stop on a trip to Far North Queensland, but for the truly adventurous, there are more stunning pockets of paradise, such as Mossman, a day trip from Cairns, further north. Beyond Mossman, a minor road services the small community of Cape Tribulation in the Daintree National Park, a spectacular, millennia-old rainforest. Here the visitor can see pristine coral cays, steamy jungles and endless, riotous vegetation. During the wet season, from November to March, the road can occasionally become impassable even in sturdy 4WDs.

Continuing north, Cooktown is the last major settlement on the east coast, perched at the edge of the pre-historic Daintree wilderness. It was here in June 1770 that Captain Cook's barque the HM *Endeavour* struck the Great Barrier Reef, forcing him to beach the vessel to carry out repairs to her hull. Getting to Cooktown, via the rugged Bloomfield Track which runs from Cape Tribulation, is not recommended for novice travellers and certainly not for anyone without a suitably geared 4WD.

Even further north, following a jaw-shuddering, bum-aching drive of some 900 kilometres, you reach Bamaga, an isolated settlement of mainly Torres Strait Islanders and Aborigines, close to the tip of Cape York. The journey is made via rough dirt tracks and tricky river crossings which are nothing but dusty riverbeds during the 'dry season' but mighty, swirling torrents during the monsoons. The actual tip of Cape York – little more than a rocky outcrop jutting out to sea – is a further 60 kilometres through a nearly unbroken canopy of virgin bush, known as the Lockerbie Rainforest. A sign proclaiming this to be the 'northernmost point on the Australian continent' is the only drawcard, but an appealing one, we noted, given the number of 4WD enthusiasts who make the trip each year.

Beyond Cape York, a maze of fractured islands dots the sea like giant stepping stones. If you were sitting on Cape York's tip, you could dip your toe in three seas and two oceans – the Cape marks the confluence of the Coral Sea to the east, the Arafura Sea and the Gulf of Carpentaria to the west, and the Torres Strait to the north. The Torres Strait is the narrow stretch of water between Australia and Papua New Guinea where the Pacific and Indian oceans converge. At its narrowest point, mainland Australia lies just 150 kilometres from its northern neighbour. It is not hard to imagine that this strait was formerly dominated by a land bridge linking the two countries. It was submerged by rising sea levels some six thousand years ago and many of the western Torres Strait Islands that jut out from the sea are the remaining peaks of the bridge.

The thrill of getting there is, of course, the main reason these enthusiasts undertake such hair-raising drives. If you think I'm overreacting, here are just some of the 'guidance' notes mentioned on one of the 4WD tour company's website for anyone bold enough to venture that far:

> *Much of the surface has no gravel. On steep slopes, or where it is red soil, it can be very slippery in wet weather. Road conditions can vary greatly – either an easy drive or impassable – although improving with new bridges over Woobadda and Bloomfield River.*
>
> *Creek/River Crossings – Normally straightforward, but in wet weather, there could be two difficult crossings. Most 4WDs can only cross up to 600 mm (2 feet) without damage – check your owner's manual. Even if capable of deeper water, strong currents can easily wash 4WDs away! Always walk into deep crossings first to determine depth and speed. If in doubt, always wait for the water to go down.* (Author's note: this advice is given to people driving through crocodile country!)
>
> *Steep Climbs and Descents – Select the correct gear and engage before the climb – If slippery, engage 4WD – make sure you know how to do this! In some vehicles, hubs must be locked beforehand.* (Author's note: locking hubs, did you say?)
>
> *Descending is often more dangerous. Select low gear beforehand, keep the speed down using engine braking where possible. Never rely on brakes alone. If you start to slide, accelerate to straighten the vehicle – braking makes the slide worse.* (Author's note: accelerating when sliding down a slippery slope seems a bit counterproductive to me, but I am no expert in this matter.)

Boggy Patches – If the surface breaks up, boggy patches can develop so try to drive on the hardest surface or follow existing ruts. Otherwise, check boggy patches before driving through. (Author's note: I can only imagine the condition of the upholstery inside the car if one were to step in and out of every muddy bog along the way.)

Unimproved Surface – Surfaces can be loose and slippery even when dry and slides can develop easily. Drive slowly and avoid hard braking or rapid acceleration. (Author's note: what happened to all the talk about the roads being in good condition during the 'dry season'?)

Dust – Can cause decreased visibility and lead to accidents, so don't stop suddenly in a dust cloud, don't follow too closely and put your headlights on so other traffic can see you. (Author's note: if I don't stop, I will get closer, won't I?)

The list of recommendations ends with one comment which makes a vain attempt to temper all preceding warnings:

An enjoyable 4WD drive if the driver is sensible and drives carefully.

Needless to say, Ambika and I were in no real hurry to go on a 4WD expedition in the wilderness any time soon.

Our bus pulled into Cairns in the pre-dawn darkness, with most of the city still fast asleep after what we guessed must have been a big Friday night. The first thing we noticed, even at 6 a.m., was the humidity, which smacked us in the face like a wet towel. Ambika and I were from Mumbai which was often humid, and we were relatively well acclimatised after spending the last few days in central Queensland, but Cairns' humidity was unlike anything we had ever experienced. At that early hour, the city appeared quiet, modern and tidy, with tree-lined avenues, a profusion of gardens and an eclectic mix of old heritage buildings nestled among examples of more modern architecture. Once again, we'd booked an Airbnb homestay, and our host Ronnie had graciously offered to pick us up from the bus stop and drive us to his house about five kilometres from the centre of town.

Ronnie's single-storey 'Queenslander' was made of solid timber and weatherboard cladding. It was perched on stilts in a traditional construction style designed to withstand flooding, high temperatures and pest infestations. The raised design also cooled the home by drawing air up from below. The house was painted white which reflected the light of the splendid tropical sun, and the edges were painted with a deep cobalt blue which added a touch of character.

The lower section of the house was modified to accommodate Airbnb guests, and this was to be our home. Our tentative plans were to stay in Cairns for a few days, exploring the city, visiting the Atherton Tablelands, and hiring a car to travel further north to Cape Tribulation. Being a mariner, I was keen to retrace Captain Cook's eventful journey along the coast, and I wanted to visit the place where his voyage and potentially the discovery of this country almost came unhinged.

Ronnie was an affable and softly-spoken man in his early sixties with a lean, athletic build and silver hair cropped short. He showed us around our one-bedroom unit and we spent a bit of time getting to know him. He told us he ran a local business grinding tree stumps. After a light breakfast and a round of laundry, we hopped on the local bus and headed into Cairns city. At the rear of the bus sat a family of Indigenous people – a middle-aged woman, an old man, a youth and two small children. The youth appeared to be in charge and did most of the talking. We watched with curiosity as they shuffled off the bus a few stops before we reached the Central Business District (CBD). It was ironic that we'd been in Australia for more than three weeks but this was the first time that we'd seen any Aborigines up close.

We asked one of the locals at a street-side café about the situation. Like many people we met on our trip, Tim, a British immigrant and a long-term resident of Cairns was knowledgeable but non-committal about the subject.

'It's a sorry state indeed. On the one hand, we acknowledge that this land belongs to the traditional owners and have made amends since the '67 referendum and the Mabo decision back in '92. Then there was Kevin Rudd's formal apology on behalf of the Australian Parliament in 2008.'

'But on the other hand, we give them government benefits with taxpayers' money, more out of a sense of obligation than with a true will to make a change. It's a complicated situation,' he added as he prepared to leave, clearly uncomfortable discussing this matter. 'But at least this time around we have our hearts in the right place.'

Tim was referring to the 1967 referendum which for the first time gave Aborigines voting and citizenship rights. Up until then, they were not considered citizens, something they – and many progressive white Australians at the time – vehemently objected to. Australia's Constitution, written in 1900, explicitly stated that Aborigines would not be counted in any state or federal census. The 1967 referendum set a voting record, with 90.77 per cent of the population voting in favour of it, a sign of the deep shame and ownership the new generation felt for the misdeeds of Australia's first settlers and subsequent governments.

Prime Minister Rudd's apology in 2008, on the other hand, was made to the 'Stolen Generations' – those Aboriginal children whose lives had been blighted by past government policies of forced removal and assimilation. The practice, established in 1905, continued well into the 1970s, during which time hundreds of thousands of children were forcibly taken from their families, most often never to see them again, and resettled in orphanages. The government actually believed that they were trying to help by positively influencing the condition of future generations. The execution of the practice, and the final outcome, however, were entirely off the mark. The profound psychological and socio-economic effects of such traumatic separations were still being felt to this day.

The inconvenient truth is that the Aborigines, the oldest surviving civilisation in the world, were doing just fine until Captain Cook came along and claimed 'Terra Australis' for the British Crown. Even Cook, despite his unsavoury interactions with the locals, made the following assessment in his journal:

> ... they may in appear to some to be the most wretched people upon the earth, but in reality, they are far more happier than we Europeans; being wholly unacquainted not only with the superfluous but the necessary conveniences so much sought in Europe, they are happy in not knowing the use of them ... the earth and sea of their own accord furnished them with all things necessary for life.

Cook's instructions, when he set sail on his voyage of exploration, were to take possession of the great southern continent if it was uninhabited, or with the consent of the natives if it was occupied. Upon his arrival, he declared Sydney's Botany Bay to be the property of Britain's King George III, in effect laying claim to the entire continent. He ignored the fact that the land was already well-populated, as was glaringly evident by the mass of Aborigines who lined the shores, watching in shocked amazement, their spears raised in a helpless show of self-defence, as the British ships arrived. Cook's failure to even attempt to gain the consent of the natives began a legal fiction and one of the world's biggest political make-believe stories that Australia was 'terra nullius' – an unoccupied land free for anyone's taking. The truth is that at the time of the first landings, nearly 750,000 Aborigines were living on the continent in almost four hundred different clans.

Of course, Australia has come a long way since then in acknowledging and accepting Aborigines as the true custodians and has taken steps to make amends. However, many critics claim it can never be enough.

Our first stop in Cairns was the famous Rusty's Markets located in the centre of the city. This all-day weekend market is a permanent fixture on the calendar, much loved by both locals and visitors. We arrived around midday and the market was abuzz with activity, heaving with patrons moving purposefully from stall to stall, hand-picking the best local produce on offer. The mood was convivial and the air suffused with the divine aromas of fresh tropical fruits, scented oils, coffee beans, spices and fragrant candles. The colourful stalls, the array of eateries – from crepe stations to satay stalls, mobile cafés to juice corners – gave Rusty's a carnival-like feel. Proudly supporting local farmers and artisans, the market represents the rich bounty of the tropics – selling exotic fruits like mangoes, ruby-red dragonfruits, luscious pineapples, and sun-ripened rambutans – as well as bounteous herbs and vegetables like fresh cabbage, onions, zucchinis and eggplants. Farmers come from as far as Innisfail and Tully to sell their produce.

The noise of commerce and idle banter was inviting, and everywhere we looked, we could see people with broad smiles eager to strike up a conversation. We were in no real hurry to leave and so after wandering around for a while, we eventually parked ourselves in one of the food stalls and had a lazy pasta lunch along with some fresh litchi juice from fruits handpicked from a local farm in Mareeba.

Later that afternoon, we took a stroll along Wharf Street and the Cairns Esplanade – the tastefully done promenade fringed by manicured gardens and shaded avenues. The Esplanade's timber decking gleamed in the sunlight as if it had been recently polished. The southern end of the boardwalk was lined with fine dining restaurants and chic bars, most of which were bustling with activity. Smartly dressed waiters in crisp white uniforms juggled trays heaped with local delicacies. Pleasure yachts of all sizes and descriptions bobbed in the sheltered waters of the marina with the occasional charter sailboat or a river cruise operator offering last-minute deals to passers-by.

The boardwalk folded in upon itself at the northern edge and followed the curve of the bay. This section was dominated by a triangular saltwater lagoon whose apex pierced the landscaped gardens. A great initiative by the council, the 4800-square metre lagoon drew water directly from Trinity Bay and provided safe swimming away from the deadly crocodiles, stinger rays and jellyfish. The weekend revellers were making the best of the beautiful afternoon, and although the place was crowded, there was a wonderful sense of community spirit. Scores of young families spread across the grassed courtyards and mingled around the barbecues. Kids were having the time of their lives in the lagoon while locals and visitors alike lounged languidly on the timber decking, soaking up the warmth of the late afternoon sun. This was a showcase of life in tropical Far North Queensland, and it was a glimpse into what I'd always imagined Australian lifestyle to be. We had a few years of uncertainty and hard work ahead of us, that was certain, but the potential rewards at the end of our struggles made it look worthwhile.

CHAPTER 12
Inside a Picture Postcard

There's no better place to find yourself than sitting by a waterfall and listening to its music – Roland R Kemler

Across the street, the Cairns Esplanade was jammed with tour company offices with the occasional fast food joints and cafés wedged in between. Tour company touts, most of whom appeared to be backpackers on work visas, scoured the streets, waylaying passers-by who were unfortunate enough to venture too close. Flashy pamphlets and glossy brochures were handed out, while last-minute deals were made on street corners in hushed tones – the interactions appearing dodgier than an amateur drug deal caught on CCTV.

Cairns was the perfect spot for exploring the Great Barrier Reef (GBR) and the range of activities on offer was endless – scuba diving, snorkelling, glass-bottom boat trips, helicopter rides, and sunset cruises. On one of the outer reefs, a sizeable floating pontoon serviced by a state-of-the-art catamaran promised viewing platforms, classy restaurants and a licensed bar.

Business was booming and the contribution that the Great Barrier Reef makes to the Australian economy was quite evident. Apart from the economic, social and iconic value of the world heritage site, the industry supported tens of thousands of jobs and raked in billions of dollars in revenue yearly.

The Great Barrier Reef is one of the seven wonders of the natural world and undoubtedly one of Australia's most remarkable natural gifts. The reef structure is beautiful both above and below the water and offers visitors some of the most spectacular scenery on Earth – a vast and captivating mosaic of reefs, islands and coral cays. The marine park stretches approximately 2300 kilometres along the Queensland coast, from the Torres Strait at the northern tip to just north of Bundaberg – roughly the same distance as Vancouver to the Mexican border – and encompasses an area of some 344,000 square kilometres. Comprising over 3000 individual systems and coral cays and over 900 picturesque tropical islands, it's truly a unique system of global significance. It wasn't until the 1970s that tourism in this region had begun to grow, but the sector boomed in the late 1980s and early 1990s with improvements to air and road transport.

Tragically, this unique and fragile ecosystem currently faces the challenges of global warming and the ravages of extreme weather. In March 2017, Cyclone Debbie, a category 4 system, made landfall at Airlie Beach, and apart from the swathe of devastation on land, the winds caused a storm surge which created widespread damage to the Reef. The usually resilient Reef colonies closest to the coast bore the brunt with large pieces of coral snapped from their bases like dry twigs. Those that managed to survive suffered bleaching and died due to extreme stress. The Reef has been experiencing coral bleaching for a while. Although the effects vary and there's no real consensus as to the exact cause and severity, the fact remains that the Reef is under threat. One economic report claimed, 'We have already lost around 50 per cent of the corals on the Great Barrier Reef in the last 30 years. Severe changes in the ocean will see a continued decline.' A grim forecast but one which hopefully we will redress. I pray – and I'm sure I echo the sentiment of people from around the world – that the beauty of the Reef does not diminish, and that someday Ambika and I might bring our kids to enjoy this very special place.

As much as we would have loved to have indulged in some reef activities, we were on a budget and running out of time. We'd been on the road for three weeks by this stage but hadn't even left Queensland. We decided to enjoy some of the natural beauty of the tropical hinterland, promising ourselves that we would return and see the Reef properly again someday.

Early the next morning we set off for the Cairns Botanic Gardens, a few kilometres north of the city. The gardens offer a spectacular introduction to the wild array of species that exist in the ancient forests of the Daintree region as well as numerous species from around the world. Split into five distinct zones, the sprawling gardens are well maintained, and the many shaded areas provide a welcome respite from the relentless heat.

The highlight of our afternoon however was picking up our rental car. In a trip already marked by many 'firsts', driving a car outside of India for the very first time was bound to be something special. This may not come across as a particularly noteworthy achievement, but for Ambika and I, it was. Having driven in Mumbai all our lives, we had unfortunately accumulated habits which would have been – putting it mildly – scoffed at elsewhere. As Sarah Macdonald, the Australian author of the bestselling book *Holy Cow*, summed it up, driving in India was a case of 'might is right'. Road rules were used merely as guidelines – only the biggest survived. Driving in Australia would be a welcome change, at least in the regional centres without too much traffic. Hopefully, we'd return the car incident-free and without any traffic infringements.

After completing the paperwork in a matter of minutes, we soon left the car park in a gleaming new silver Hyundai hatchback, complete with a portable GPS device. For a celebratory run, we drove to Palm Cove, about thirty minutes from Cairns. This charming little coastal town, draped with tropical lushness and bordering the azure waters of the Coral Sea, is a prime holiday destination featuring a range of waterfront resorts as well as some breathtakingly beautiful private bungalows with sprawling gardens and fantastic sea views.

It was nearing sunset by the time we got there and there weren't too many people on the main beach as there was a stiff north-easterly. We watched a flock of plump seagulls battling the winds, flapping their wings, desperately trying to get home before nightfall. Here and there holidaying couples strolled hand in hand along the promenade, soaking up the last vestiges of the tropical sun.

Two warning signs were displayed prominently at the main entrance to the beach. One warned of crocodiles and for people to be extremely cautious – even at the water's edge. The other sign reminded beachgoers that this was jellyfish territory, although they wouldn't start to appear until the warm summer months of October to March. Rated as one of the most lethal creatures in the animal kingdom, the harmless-looking, delicate Irukandji jellyfish inject the unwary beachgoer with a highly poisonous venom from thousands of their microscopic barbed stingers. The pain, so I'm told, is excruciating and sometimes people do not recover from the shock. The recommended first aid is to pour vinegar over the affected area, and there was a large can placed in a retainer just below the sign for this specific purpose.

We spent the rest of the afternoon by the beachfront – well away from the water's edge – enjoying a meal of fish and chips while watching the tropical sunset paint the eastern skies a kaleidoscope of vivid colours. In a world facing the ever-increasing challenges of global warming, overpopulation, consumerism, border infiltration, terrorism, and a range of other socio-economic problems, Australia seemed to offer a refreshing break from the chaos. Somehow, people here could still afford to slow down and enjoy life's simple pleasures – a relaxed chat with a total stranger, a walk along a quiet suburban street without the fear of being mugged, or a meal of fish and chips beside a nearly-empty tropical beach.

Back at our Airbnb house that evening, Ronnie stopped by for a chat to check how we were doing. We told him we were having a great time and planned to visit Kuranda, a scenic village in the hills near Cairns which had a must-do cable car ride. The next day would probably be our last and we'd decided to base ourselves in Port Douglas as we explored Cape Tribulation and the Daintree Rainforest.

Ronnie suggested some local sights worth visiting and showed us photos on his phone. As he was shuffling through the images, one, in particular, caught our eye. At first glance, it appeared to be a heavily photoshopped image of a waterfall. It was not very big but it was spellbindingly beautiful, framed on all sides by lush green overgrowth with the water cascading silently into a large basin. Ronnie told us the image was real and was of the Millaa Millaa Falls in the Atherton Tablelands, about 100 kilometres from Cairns. Ambika and I cast sideways glances at each other, knowing that we had to go there. Kuranda could wait.

The Atherton Tablelands form part of the Great Dividing Range and cover an area of some 64,768 square kilometres. The Tablelands' cooler climate means there's a wide variety of landscapes and attractions – from fertile plains, rolling hills and waterfalls to expansive national parks and coffee plantations. Although the region was initially exploited for its tin and gold deposits in the 1870s, the mining boom was short-lived, and today the region's main industries are dairy, poultry and agriculture. Crops grown include bananas, sugar cane, corn/maize, avocadoes, strawberries, macadamia nuts, mangoes and citrus fruits – a veritable food bowl. In a region rich in natural beauty, the one melody that reigns supreme is the soothing sound of water. You can hear it in the gushing tones of the creeks, the lilting melodies of the countless rivulets that run through the open fields, in the cascading waterfalls and the soul-cleansing rhythm of the pouring rain.

Eager to see as much of the region as we could in a single day, I jumped online and chalked out a rough itinerary. With a drive of roughly 500 kilometres up to the Tablelands and back, plus a range of parks, waterfalls and tourist spots to visit, we wouldn't get back to Cairns until well past sunset. It was daunting but it seemed achievable.

Then I made the mistake of switching on the TV and our plan for the next day almost came undone.

A documentary about the influential '5:2 diet', popularised by British journalist and doctor Michael Mosley, was showing. The diet suggests that the human body responds well to five days' eating – and two days' fasting each week. Weight loss is just one of the many benefits and most people who'd been on the diet report a marked improvement in general health and vitality. It sounded so good Ambika and I decided to do a fast the very next day ... a busy day of driving and sightseeing activity. We were partly driven by our efforts to minimise our expenses: going hungry for a day when trying out a new diet seemed like a win-win. So confident were we of our ability to survive without a single meal that we didn't even bother to take a pack of biscuits or a piece of fruit.

We set off early southbound along the Bruce Highway. Our first stop was Babinda Boulders, just off the highway, about 60 kilometres from Cairns. The Boulders is a popular swimming and picnic area in the foothills of Mount Bartle Frere, Queensland's highest peak (admittedly at 1622 metres not that high by world standards, but this was the flattest continent, after all). The two-kilometre walk from the car park takes you through lush tropical rainforest dense with trees, ferns, vines, fungi, moss and lichen. The region has one of the highest rainfalls in the country, and the day we visited the creek gushed with the constant flow of sparkling, cold, clear water from the mountain.

Our next stop was the scenic Josephine Falls a further 20 kilometres on, also fed from the same mountain source. This area marked the eastern edge of the expansive Wooroonooran National Park and offered a welcome respite for locals who wanted a picnic or a swim in the cool waters. Wandering amid the native gum and paperbark trees, and giant ferns and cycads, I could not help but feel overjoyed to be a part of this unspoilt landscape that was so easily accessible yet so pristine and beautiful. I suppose it all came down to statistics. With such a small and sparse population, visitor numbers to these parks are a fraction of what they'd be anywhere else in the world. Despite this, the upkeep, the recreational features and the focus on safety were second to none. We found this to be true even in the remotest tourist Australian sights – a credit to the parks and wildlife authorities who do such a stellar job.

We were soon on the road again. By now we had come to realise that Australians celebrate and encourage outdoor living, but the tourism advertisements don't do the magic justice. Taking off my tourist hat and donning my 'local resident' hat, I tried to imagine visiting these parks in our campervan along with our children in a few years. I saw us spending lazy afternoons fishing the creeks, exploring the forests and gullies, mastering our barbecuing skills and having the time of our lives. It was a heart-warming and dream-worthy goal indeed and one which was now starting to feel achievable.

It was midday by the time we took the turn-off at Innisfail and headed up the Palmerston Highway into the Tablelands. We passed vast maize fields with corn stalks billowing in the wind and fertile banana plantations, the trees sagging under their rich bounty. We saw large farmhouses and even larger sheds surrounded by acres upon acres of well-tended farmland. On some farms, we could see cattle grazing peacefully in the distance, while farmers chugged along in their tractors. It was misty, and overhead, battle-grey clouds crowded the expansive skies with the promise of rain.

We reached the first waterfall in the Tablelands' 'circuit', in the quaint little town of Millaa, population two hundred and fifty, around lunchtime. The four other falls in the circuit include the exotically named Mungalli, Elinjaa, Zillie and Pepina falls. Nestled 2900 feet above sea level, Millaa Millaa took our breath away – the photo we saw on Ronnie's phone was no exaggeration. The waterfall and the surrounding landscape were utterly spell-binding, the delicate fawn-like beauty and perfect symmetry suggesting fairies with divine powers must have crafted the unique masterpiece! The waterfall was by no means the highest or the biggest in the region, but what it lacked in size it more than made up for in aesthetics. The water was cool and a few people were swimming, but we just dipped our feet up to our ankles and sat by the waterfall for a while.

On the way back to Cairns, we visited the Mount Hypipamee Crater – a 70-metre-wide hole known as a 'diatreme' thought to have formed by a volcanic gas explosion thousands of years ago. The crater had sheer granite walls and a deep cavity filled with water 60 metres from the surface and covered with green mossy native seaweed. We also saw the famous Curtain Fig Tree in Yungaburra – a 500-year-old 'strangler' fig which had devoured its host tree centuries ago and stood at a uniquely weird forty-five-degree angle with its aerial roots dropping 15 metres to the ground in one long continuous curtain.

Our eventful day was nearing its end and with dusk soon approaching we were in a hurry to get back to Cairns. By this stage, the effects of our fasting had well and truly hit and we both had splitting headaches and were nauseous, although neither of us was willing to admit it! The twisty and winding road down to the coast only added to our misery. As luck would have it, we got into Cairns around 9 p.m. and most of the fast-food outlets were closed. Ambika didn't care and had just enough energy to jump straight into bed. I munched on an apple before joining her immediately after.

We awoke early the next morning, looked at each other sheepishly, but refrained from any conversation until we'd had a hearty breakfast of eggs, baked beans and toast. Later, with our bellies full, we made a solemn vow that we would never again try any newfangled diet while travelling.

Our time well spent in Cairns, we had to move on. We were not done with Queensland just yet, as we were headed further north deep into jungle territory – the millennia-old rainforests of Cape Tribulation beckoned.

CHAPTER 13

Where the Rainforest meets the Reef

It's the colours, the light, the space. It's really very deep in my soul ... In the Australian bush and inland deserts, there is a sense of being the first person in a place – Suzanne Cory

The Captain Cook Highway snaked north, hugging the coastline, never far from glorious views of the azure waters of the Coral Sea and the off-lying reefs and islands. We drove with the windows down, breathing in the briny smell of the sea and the earthy scents of the forested foreshore. It was another beautiful day with a warm tropical sun shining brightly in a cobalt blue sky. The traffic was light, and we were looking for excuses to pull over at every opportunity to prolong the experience. We were in no real hurry to reach Port Douglas.

As we crossed the Barron River, we noticed numerous narrow and solitary roads branching off the highway. Each one, it turned out, led to a cove that offered the visitor a private slice of paradise. While the quaintly named Yorkeys Knob was popular with mariners visiting Cairns, Trinity Beach catered mainly to local families. Palm Cove, on the other hand, had boutique attractions that lured richer holidaymakers. And Ellis Beach was a well-known hippie enclave where campers could enjoy a 'no frills' experience.

We reached the alluring town of Port Douglas late in the afternoon. We had decided to base ourselves here for a couple of days while we explored the Daintree region and Cape Tribulation. Our Airbnb hosts, Sian and Nolan, lived in a cosy two-bedroom townhouse in a stylish gated complex in one of the quiet, leafy suburbs off Four Mile Beach. Sian told us beforehand that they would not be at home when we arrived, so she'd made arrangements for us to collect the keys and settle in.

We were no longer surprised at this sort of trusting attitude, but the gratitude we felt and the responsibility that came with it never diminished. Backpacking teaches you many things and one of them is to take measured chances in dealing with your fellow human beings. The more you trust your instincts, the better your ability to sense danger. I've always lived my life with a measure of faith sprinkled with a dash of caution, and thus far this has held me in good stead. I've met many wonderful people, some of whom have become life-long friends.

Sian and Nolan's house was chic and compact and tastefully adorned with minimalist furniture and bric-a-brac from around the world. Every detail in the house spoke of travel and wild escapes. The late afternoon sunlight pouring in through the windows bathed the living room in a soft golden hue. The most striking of all the items on display were the photographs and collages that adorned the walls and the countertops. The pictures depicted a beautiful couple basking in perpetual happiness, joined by their equally playful dogs.

Our hosts had laid out one of the corner bedrooms for our stay, a small yet stylish space with an en suite bathroom. On a little side table near the window sat a fruit basket, a kettle, milk and other breakfast condiments. This particular Airbnb listing indicated that guests did not have access to the kitchen. A minor inconvenience compensated by the perfect location.

Sian and Nolan arrived home just as we were preparing to head out for a stroll by the beach. They were in their early twenties, friendly and unassuming with an aura of tranquillity about them, probably an outward reflection based on their years of travel. Their two playful Labradors, Vonnegut and Hemmingway, wasted no time getting to know us and smothered us with their big furry embrace and inquisitive wet muzzles.

Sian worked part-time at a wildlife habitat centre in Port Douglas while she was studying for her Masters in Humanities at university. She had the most disarming smile which lit up the room. Nolan's unkempt hair and short unruly beard gave him the appearance of a castaway, but his warm and friendly personality shone through. He told us he worked as a paralegal for a private law firm in Port Douglas.

After a quick chat, we took off for a walk around the leafy and upmarket neighbourhood. In no time at all, we found ourselves at Four Mile Beach – a four-kilometre stretch of unspoilt paradise rated as one of the best known and most popular in northern Australia. Forming a lazy arc from the base of the prominent 70-metre-high Island Point, the beach ends among the scattered reefs at the Mowbray River mouth. It's comparable with the colourful Copacabana in Brazil or the iconic Palm Beach in Florida but, unlike its glitzy counterparts, the day we visited it was free from crowds and irksome tour operators. It seemed completely untouched, and we had it all to ourselves, with just a few locals ambling along the foreshore on their evening walks.

From a sleepy seaside town in the 1970s, by the late 1980s, Port Douglas had become a premium tourist destination. It was one of those places that was just picture-perfect. The landscape appeared digitally photoshopped – every mountain top perfectly crowned, every coconut tree perfectly angled and the curve of the beach created as if with architectural precision. It's the kind of place which grabs you and makes you want to stay forever.

It certainly had that effect on Beatrice, an elderly lady whom we met on the beach that afternoon.

'I moved here twenty years ago from Melbourne. I was going through a messy divorce and needed some time off. A friend of mine who owns a studio in Cairns recommended the move, and that's what I did. But I just fell in love with the slow pace, the natural beauty and the tranquil lifestyle.'

Donovan, a waiter we met at a café that evening, had a similar take. 'I was a twenty-year-old Perth-based bloke fresh out of university. Instead of the customary round-the-world trip that most of my mates took as a rite of passage, I decided to explore my own country. After a three-month road trip, I landed in Port Douglas and what was meant to be the last stop in my itinerary turned out to be my final destination. I've been here for over five years now and am absolutely in love with the culture and pristine beauty of the place. Secret back roads to ancient rainforests, hidden waterfalls, miles of secluded beaches – you don't get a free ticket to paradise twice in your life!' he added, as he winked conspiratorially while he cleared the coffee mugs.

The region is also home to one of the oldest living cultures in the world – the Kuku Yalanji tribe, who have been living in harmony in the rainforests for over 50,000 years. Coming face to face with an Indigenous person from this clan today would be surreal. It would be a bit like chancing upon a pyramid construction site in Egypt where labourers are hard at work building a mammoth tomb for the reigning pharaoh! Imagine walking up to the lead architect and discussing the finer details of the project and asking him how he managed to get that nine-ton block up to the pinnacle! As fanciful as this encounter may seem, these workers would still be 45,000 years younger than the Aborigines in Australia.

Pete, an enthusiastic seventy-year-old war veteran and volunteer at the visitor centre, gave us some more insight when we stopped by for some maps and brochures. 'The traditional owners of the land once lived in a much wider region that spread from Port Douglas, Cooktown and Chillagoe in the west. The Kuku Yalanji began concentrating around the Mossman River area after World War II. The islands, beaches, creek mouths, backing dunes and lowland rainforest of the Daintree area provided them with sustenance, and they led a hunter-gatherer lifestyle on a systematic, seasonal and cultural basis. Most of the surviving members still adhere to the same guiding principles today.

'You might have seen one famous face in the Australian media.' Pete pointed to a music CD by Jessica Mauboy. 'Jessica's half-Indigenous and her mother belongs to the Kuku Yalanji tribe.'

Mauboy represented the new wave of talented Indigenous Australians who were finding a voice in mainstream Australia, be it politics, sports, arts or education.

Just over three thousand people call Port Douglas home though these numbers swell during the peak tourist season or big local events. The town has a range of accommodation options, from budget hotels and homestay apartments to world-class resorts like the Sheraton Grand Mirage and the Niramaya Villas & Spa that take luxury to the next level. Port Douglas shot to international fame in 1996 when then US President Bill Clinton and First Lady Hillary chose it as their only holiday destination during a visit to Australia. They loved the place so much that they returned in 2001. It was here, while dining at a local restaurant, that Clinton was advised of the 9/11 terrorist attacks.

Walking along Macrossan Street that evening, we began to appreciate the Australian spirit of 'mateship', where the line between the super-rich and the shoe-string-budget traveller blurs into insignificance. Take-away diners and unassuming local pubs comfortably rubbed shoulders with Michelin-starred restaurants. Sharing the same latitude as Tahiti, Port Douglas retains an old-fashioned charm with its wide, shaded lanes, rustic colonial homes and century-old establishments. In true Australian fashion, this town was not an exclusive millionaire's retreat, although it had great potential to be one: it was a place where the super-rich could wear cheap hats and casual beachwear and mingle with the locals without concern.

We reached the wharf and park which mark the town's perimeter and offer captivating views of the Coral Sea. The undulating mountain ranges of the Daintree National Park served as a stunning backdrop. Somewhere, beyond those lofty ranges, the Great Dividing range flattens out into the vast expanse of the Cape York Peninsula – Far North Queensland's final frontier. The region beyond is a wild outback territory known as the Savannah Gulf, a land that stretches to the Gulf of Carpentaria – an ancient area brimming with geological wonders, historic mining towns and unspoilt natural beauty.

Port Douglas also marks the spot where Australia's most-loved adventurer, conservationist and explorer, Steve Irwin, died in September 2006. With his signature khaki shorts, infectious enthusiasm and distinctly Australian colloquialism – especially his use of the word 'crikey' – Steve won the heart of millions of people around the world in the hit television series *Crocodile Hunter*. I remember watching his wildlife shows when I was growing up. To me, he represented the quintessential Australian – witty and unassuming with a love of adventure and the outdoors.

Steve's childlike curiosity and passion were incomparable, and people instantly fell in love with him. His wife, Terri, once called him an 'environmental Tarzan and a larger-than-life superhero'. Seldom do you find a television personality with such international appeal; someone so charismatic they connect with audiences all around the world. Steve was one of my role models when I was growing up. Little did I know that I would someday migrate to Australia and have my own adventures in 'crocodile country'.

Later that evening, we took a drive to Island Point Road, a steep incline which culminates at the Trinity Bay Lookout. From this vantage point, you have a magnificent and uninterrupted view of Four Mile Beach and its white coral sands backed by swaying palm trees. Towards sunset we made our way to the waterfront park where groups of tourists and locals were scattered about, far enough apart to enjoy the view in peace. Young families picnicked on the grass while kids ran wild in the play area. Backpackers huddled up in groups of twos and threes sharing their experiences of life on the road or striking up conversations in a bid to make new friends. Out on the water, sailboats, cruisers and small skiffs rounded the Island Point bend at a leisurely pace, some heading out for a sunset cruise, most others inbound after a day of fishing and reef activity.

I will always cherish that particular sunset because it was at this spot that Ambika and I lamented the loss of our dads, both of whom had died in quick succession just twelve months earlier.

For both of us, 2013 was a tough one – a year of spectacular highs and soul-sapping lows when our dads died. At the time, we were busy with our marriage preparations, counting down to what was meant to be the happiest day of our lives. We were robbed of an opportunity to mourn for them as we were busy dealing with a lot at that time – our visa applications, the wedding plans, and my impending sea voyage.

I barely got to know my dad when I was growing up. An expat in the Middle East, he worked as an electrical supervisor and foreman for a company in Saudi Arabia for much of his life. He'd be gone for a year at a time only to return home for a month's holiday. He was a kind of demigod to me, with his bulging muscles and striking personality. I was in awe of him and failed to notice that he had a soft side too, a side that wanted to connect with his children above everything else. As fate decreed, I began my sea career just as he retired.

Fortunately, unlike Dad, I was home more often, and I often stayed for a couple of months at a time in between shipboard assignments. It was during this period that I got to spend time with him at our family home in a tiny hamlet on the outskirts of Udipi in the southern state of Karnataka. Papa, as I fondly called him, was more a friend to me than a parent. Despite our considerable age difference, there were never any barriers. In between ship voyages and solo backpacking treks, he taught me the art of simple living, gave me the courage to face life's toughest challenges and instilled in me the virtues of persistence and patience.

My dad had a heart of gold and was one of the few people I knew who practised the art of unconditional love and selfless service without any effort. He instilled in me a keen sense of adventure and the confidence to be self-reliant. A quiet non-conformist, he was a bit of a misfit and never did things based on social consensus. In my early thirties and showing no interest in getting married or settling down, he told me that it would happen when the time was right. I knew deep down he wanted me to marry someone who would bring me happiness, but not once did he ever say so. That all changed when Ambika came into my life in late 2012, breaking through my defences, much to my amazement and my father's delight. It did not take long – although, from Ambika's perspective, it took forever – for me to propose. My dad had picked up that I was very fond of her. He told me later on that it was evident in the way I dressed up whenever I went out on a date with her and the lengthy phone conversations we would have.

Papa was there the day I proposed to Ambika. I was about to join my next ship and had finally mustered the courage to propose. I considered a lot of romantic ways to do it but, in the end, chose to include our nearest and dearest. After all the agony I'd put Ambika and our families through due to my prolonged indecision, it only seemed fair.

Early in January of 2013, a few days before I was about to embark on my next ship, I devised a plan to surprise Ambika with the help of her brother, Gaurav. On the appointed day Gaurav was tasked with bringing our parents to Mount Mary Basilica, a holy shrine atop a hillock in the swanky suburb of Bandra, in Mumbai. Directly across the Basilica on the western side is a beautiful Oratory with grand views of the Arabian Sea. Its dual staircases lead to a six-and-half-foot marble statue of Mother Mary serenely holding a rosary in her hands. At night, the glow emanating from the burning of wax offerings atop this shrine is visible from afar. This was one of Ambika's favourite spots in Mumbai, and she would visit the shrine occasionally to light a candle and experience the stillness. It seemed like the perfect setting for a proposal that appeared to have occurred by divine intervention.

On the assigned day, I asked Ambika out on a date and had arranged to meet her at a cafe located near the shrine. Unbeknownst to her, Gaurav had gathered our family members – who had figured out the plot by now - within the foregrounds of the Basilica. After a leisurely chat, Ambika and I casually sauntered up in the general direction of the Oratory. Ambika was still completely unaware of what was soon to unfold. I timed it to perfection; as we climbed up the final step and paused to offer a prayer at the feet of Our Lady, I casually pulled out a diamond ring from my pocket and got down on one knee, and looking deep into her eyes with all my conviction asked Ambika to marry me. For those few minutes it felt as if time stood still; my heart was thumping louder than jungle drums, and my legs were quivering with nervousness. Ambika, on the other hand, was tongue-tied and stared at me with a stunned look, trying to process what was going on. And then, just as she had recovered enough to say 'Yes', our parents, who were watching the unfolding drama, came out of hiding, cheering in unison. Ambika, who was still in a state of shock, looked as if she would faint any second when she saw our folks huddled together at the bottom of the stairs.

My dad, ever the quiet one, was beaming from ear to ear on that day. I remember him hugging Ambika tightly, saying almost half-jokingly, 'I will now not mind bidding adieu to this life, because I know that Jason is in good hands.'

From that moment on, life accelerated. Ambika and I busied ourselves with the marriage preparations and migration plans. My dad, who had been diagnosed with prostate cancer a few months prior, was given a clean chit post-surgery. He was, however, slowing down and his health was deteriorating. I failed to recognise the signs that he was slowly fading away. Just a few weeks before the wedding, he suffered a massive heart attack and died. The only consolation for me was the fact that I was at his side when he breathed his last.

Ambika's father, whom I got to know briefly during our courtship, was likewise softly-spoken and gentle. Baba (meaning dad), as he was lovingly called in Bengali, had a rare heart condition since birth and his poor health in recent years had restricted his movements. My dad would often visit Ambika's home and spend time with her father. They developed a good friendship in the short time they got to know each other. The grief of my dad's passing still fresh in our hearts, yet buoyed by our marriage, we were looking forward to our new life together. But fate dealt us with another cruel blow just three days after our wedding when Ambika's dad too suddenly passed away of heart failure. We were completely devastated and it took all of our reserves to pull each other out from the depths of despair.

That evening in Port Douglas, on the eve of the first anniversary of my father's death, as we sat by the water's edge watching the crimson sun dip below the mountain ranges, I finally said a proper goodbye to his soul. There were no tears, as time had served to cushion the blow. I did not feel sorrow but immense gratitude for having had the opportunity to have known him. In his characteristic way, I imagined him smiling down on me saying, 'Son, I've lived my life to the fullest. Now go have your own adventures!'

CHAPTER 14
Shipwrecked

Do not follow where the path may lead. Go instead where there is no path and leave a trail – Ralph Waldo Emerson

'Work those pumps, men ... for God's sake keep at it if you want to see the light of day!' I could just imagine the boatswain shouting orders as the ship started listing to one side. It was riding up higher on the coral reef on the receding tide, and the cold dark waters were seeping into the holds, the water levels rising by the minute. It was 11 p.m. on 10 June 1770. The fate of HM *Endeavour*, the success of the entire voyage – and potentially the discovery of Australia itself – now lay in the expert hands of Captain James Cook and his crew.

Being a seafarer, I related to their distress, but my navigational skills pale in comparison with those pioneers and explorers from that bygone era. Still, I pictured the abject terror that would have seized them as the ship's hull grated against the sharp edges of the coral reef. I imagined the first few moments of utter disbelief and inaction of the senior officers. Twenty miles from land and knowing that the depths reduced from twenty fathoms to zero in no time at all, Cook would have been acutely aware that this was no gentle sandy spit he'd run aground on.

I could feel the pressure mounting on the captain, as if I were on the bridge with him. Cook knew that trying to float the ship might prove disastrous, with there being every possibility the jagged coral would slice through the hull with any further movement. But he also dreaded the possibility of becoming stranded in the middle of nowhere. With a stoic disposition, he and his men decided to do whatever they could to get the *Endeavour* afloat.

Over the next thirteen hours the crew worked relentlessly to keep the ship afloat, guns and provisions were thrown overboard, anchors were run out, and capstans heaved in a bid to pry the ship free. The bilge pumps were operated non-stop. Finally, at around 10.30 a.m., with the crew exhausted from the efforts through the night, there was a glimmer of hope as the onrush of the returning tide lapped over the edge of the coral and began rocking the ship back and forth. Inch by laborious inch, the windlass and capstan heaved the vessel forward, and the *Endeavour* finally broke free and entered deeper waters.

Once out of immediate harm's way, one of the midshipmen, Mr Monkhouse, experimented with the use of a 'fothering' technique, sliding a large piece of canvas filled with loose clumps of oakum, wool and sheep dung across the ship's bottom, the suction effectively carrying the 'filth' into the cavity and plugging the leak.

With resurgent hope, Cook managed to sail the boat into a narrow channel at the mouth of a river, landing it at a secluded spot on the mangrove-infested swamp banks. He would later name this waterway the Endeavour River in honour of his barque. On 18 June, once the ship had been securely docked on a makeshift wooden stage, the carpenters set to work. To their astonishment, they found a hole big enough to have sunk a vessel with double the number of pumps. Somehow, as if by divine providence, a large piece of coral had found its way into the gaping hole, stemming the inflow of water and possibly saving the *Endeavour* from total destruction.

The landscape Cook and his crew found themselves in were one of stony hills, salt-infused mangrove swamps and scrubby, inedible trees. They noticed strange native animals but lacked the necessary skills to catch them. The natives they encountered, on the other hand, had mastered the art of hunting and fishing and appeared to live a life of abundance. A barter system was trialled, but the natives were unimpressed with the crew's offerings, having no use for glass beads, mirrors, cloth and trinkets.

During one of the many surveys of the area made aboard the ship's longboats, Cook chanced upon giant green turtles basking on a reef. Joseph Banks, the ship's official botanist and naturalist, recorded the relief and elation felt by the crew at this discovery, noting in his journal that, 'the promise of … provisions made our situation appear much less dreadful. Were we obliged to wait here for another season of the year when the winds might alter, we could do it without fear of wanting provisions: this thought alone put everybody in vast spirits.' By 15 July, Banks was gloating that 'we may now be said to swim in Plenty': the turtles were abundant, weighed between 200 to 300 pounds each, and were filled with meat and nutritious oil. It didn't take the natives very long to notice that the *Endeavour*'s decks were crawling with enough turtles to feed their clans for months.

On 19 July, the ship received a formal visitation from ten naked warriors armed with spears. When Cook refused to hand over even a single turtle, a fight ensued, and the natives lit a fire in an attempt to raze Cook's camp. Cook retaliated by ordering the firing of a musket loaded with birdshot which wounded one of the natives. This was the first shot fired on Australian soil and was a watershed moment. What the Europeans failed to understand was that turtle meat formed the staple diet for the natives. They lived in perfect balance with nature, hunting and foraging only as much as required – a key to their survival. Banks noted that 'they seemed to set no value upon anything we had except our turtles, which of all things we were the least able to spare them.'

Captain Cook had no idea when he set sail from Botany Bay in May 1770 that he was soon to encounter the largest coral reef formation in the world. The first hint of what was in store occurred around 20 May, some two weeks after leaving Botany Bay, when he was confronted with a long 'shoal' projecting eastward from a finger of land he called Sandy Cape. He'd already sighted lines of breakers which indicated undersea obstacles on several occasions and the astute navigator noticed the behavioural change in the vessel as it entered smoother waters. But he had no way of knowing that this was the sheltering effects of the Swain Reef, a collection of massive, deep-water aggregations of coral some 100 nautical miles to the east that marked the south-eastern outer reef boundary of the lagoon.

Cook was effectively sailing into a maze which constricted the seaway closer to the coast the further north he progressed. Eyes set firmly on the mainland with a focus on documenting every peak and ridge the *Endeavour* passed, he failed to identify any potential dangers on his starboard side towards the sea. If he had done so, he would have seen the sand and coral cays of the Capricornia Island group, thirty miles off the mainland, and this probably would have been a sign of the trouble that lay ahead. Even the recurring 'shoals' surrounding the Whitsunday Islands initially caused the navigator no real alarm. The irritating yet manageable shoal-dodging continued as the *Endeavour* sailed in a slow zigzag course, the captain confident of the capability of the vessel and the crew who were sounding the depths continuously. On 9 June, they anchored near a small inlet slightly east of a rocky eminence that Cook named Point Grafton.

It was to be their last night of rest for some time.

After six weeks repairing the *Endeavour* following their grounding, Cook and his crew were eager to be on their way. But first he had to somehow find a safe route out of the maze that stretched in all directions as far as the eye could see. Banks rightly described it as a 'labyrinth of shoals'. Cook decided a longboat should go first with the *Endeavour* to follow. But in which direction should he go? Sailing south, back where they came from, was not an option given the opposing trade winds. Sailing north, the most logical route, was fraught with unknown dangers. It would have to be east, sailing as far away from the mainland and hopefully finding an escape route. He gave the orders to proceed along the short channel hoping to reach the open sea, rather than risk being locked in by the Reef for eternity. On 13 August, the longboat shepherded the *Endeavour* and her crew through the narrow passage, sounding the depths frequently as they skirted the shallow waters until at last Cook found a small opening at the outer reef edge. The vessel was soon wallowing in a large south-easterly swell – a sure sign that they'd made it to deeper waters beyond the coral reef.

On 22 August 1770 Cook eventually completed his voyage along Australia's east coast. Upon reaching Possession Island in the Torres Strait, he planted the British flag and claimed the entire east coast of Australia in the name of King George III. The monarch of the British Empire had just added one of the most magnificent jewels to his crown.

After a quick breakfast, we set off for Cape Tribulation. The Daintree region encompasses a 95-square-kilometre area which starts at Mossman Gorge, continues past Daintree Village, across the Daintree River, through the rainforest of Daintree National Park to Cape Tribulation and along the Bloomfield Track towards Cooktown. The region is bounded to the west by the stunning forested hills of the MacDonnell Ranges, while to the east, the land is hemmed by a pristine coastline dotted with peaceful beaches.

The sealed road ends abruptly at the Daintree River crossing where a ferry takes you across the river and into the misty embrace of the ancient Cape Tribulation rainforest. Cape Tribulation's history started one hundred and twenty million years ago, give or take a couple of million years depending on which book you read, when the ancient landmass of Gondwana was covered in dense rainforests and inhabited by dinosaurs. Around fifty-five million years ago, Gondwana split into several pieces and the piece that we now know as Australia drifted south. Due to its isolation, and spared the ravages of climate change and ice ages, these rainforests survived and thrived. Sadly, the same can't be said for the dinosaurs.

For us, the most fascinating thing about the rainforest wasn't its age or the fact that it had barely changed in a hundred million years, but that people were stumbling upon new plant species and other exotic biological discoveries to this very day. Take the *Idiospermum australiense*, also known as 'the idiot fruit tree'. Thought to have become extinct millions of years ago, the seed was rediscovered in 1971 when a local farmer's cows became ill after having eaten the toxic fruit. Who knows how many more secrets lay hidden in the lofty reaches of the tall conifers or the mulchy undergrowth that covered the forest floor?

As we waited patiently for our ferry, I wondered what it must have been like back in the early 1900s when the first European settlers arrived. What motivated them to come here? What did they imagine they'd find in the wilderness? What hardships did they face? How fascinating, yet equally daunting, it must have been to have come face to face for the very first time with some of the world's zaniest creatures: a rat kangaroo, a Boyd's forest dragon or a spotted-tail quoll.

Isolation, wild weather and hard physical labour were not the only challenges the first settlers faced. On land, there were the mighty cassowaries – giant, flightless birds with a shy demeanour but curious disposition – while in the waters, huge estuarine crocodiles were a constant threat. The first school that opened in 1899 had to be shut within a year because the teacher unceremoniously resigned, sick of having to row his boat sixteen long and gruelling miles (four of those miles in the open sea) each day just to get to work. In time, the region had a store, post office, drapery, butcher, baker, café, blacksmith and sawmill office.

As we drove north after alighting the ferry, the change in scenery was striking. Farmland and cultivated fields on the opposite side of the river gave way to dense, untamed undergrowth. Overhead, the canopy of trees soon blocked out the sky, and there was an all-pervading dampness characteristic of the rainforest. Every now and then, the sun's rays broke through the sagging boughs of the ancient trees, giving the landscape a warm, ethereal feel. It was easy to forget that we were actually quite close to the coast.

It wasn't long before we drove past the Rainforest Village convenience store, the last fuel stop until Cooktown, 120 kilometres to the north. The sealed road however only extended to the Cape Tribulation beach house so that was as far as we could go in our rental car. Not long after passing the convenience store, we saw a young backpacker thumbing for a lift. We stopped more out of curiosity than concern.

Emma was a French backpacker on her way to Cooktown. But in her loose top, short skirt and flimsy bathroom slippers, it was hard to imagine she'd last more a few kilometres on the rough dirt track! Her black and grey Quechua backpack was overflowing, and in one hand she lugged a collapsible tent. Needless to say, she jumped straight into the back seat as soon as we pulled up. We were keen to hear about her adventures, wondering how she came to be in this remote part of Australia all by herself, on foot with nothing more than a backpack and a tent.

Emma told us she was a university student in France currently on a 'gap year'. She was funding her trip around Australia by doing casual work on rural farms and had recently spent a few weeks in Mareeba, in the Atherton Tablelands, working in an avocado farm. She'd already traversed some of the most remote regions in Australia.

'The real magic of the country only surfaces in the harsh wilderness of the outback,' she said. 'It's an intangible force which takes hold of you. It's reflected in the red mountain ranges at sunset and in the inky black sky and the million shimmering stars. You go in with a lot of fear and apprehension, but once you experience the outback, you come back a changed person.'

'I've heard some people don't come back at all,' I said half-jokingly yet alluding to the fact that every year some people went missing in outback Australia. Most of them were overseas tourists who were either unprepared or simply chose to ignore the warning signs or heed the local advice.

'What about snakes and creepy crawlies?' Ambika asked, shuddering at the very thought. 'Were you never afraid of them entering the tent while you were asleep?'

'Hasn't happened to me yet,' Emma said. 'I did have a curious wallaby chew on my tent one time. The cheeky little scoundrel damaged a large section of it, and I had to improvise with some duct tape.'

We stopped at the parking lot by the Dubuji boardwalk near Cape Tribulation. As Emma had no particular plans other than hitching a ride to Cooktown, she decided to accompany us. The boardwalk twists and turns through the lush lowland forests shaded by a canopy of enormous vines, fan palms and strangler figs. The mangrove swamps with their tippy-toe roots crowd the beachfront and offer a classic castaway backdrop.

The beach was secluded with not a soul in sight. Looking north we could just make out the faint edges of Cape Tribulation, the rocky promontory so named by Captain Cook.

'So, which countries have you visited?' I asked Emma.

'Loads of places in Europe, and also South-East Asia and India. Do you know what? Of all the places I've visited, India remains by far one of my favourite destinations.'

Emma had spent three months in India and was blown away by the sheer number of people, the cacophony of sounds and the chaos which reigned on the streets in most parts of the country. But beneath the mad rush, she began to appreciate the real beauty of the place and was charmed by its diversity. She fell in love with the vibrant colours, the endless choice of food and the stunning natural beauty. Most of all, she fell in love with the multitude of cultures that seem to co-exist in perfect harmony.

She even took some Bollywood dance lessons while in Mumbai. She was so enamoured by the whole song and dance routine of Indian cinema that she continued after she returned to France. To prove her point, she jumped up and broke into a swirl and twirl routine right there on the beach! Not one to be left behind, Ambika eagerly joined in. I found myself sitting on a twisted tree trunk watching a choreographed dance sequence from my home country. Of all the things I imagined I would see in Cape Tribulation, two beautiful women doing a Bollywood number on the sandy shores of a desolate beach was not one of them!

CHAPTER 15

Daal, Roti and War Stories

Blessed are the curious for they will have many adventures
– Unknown

Having ticked off Cape Tribulation from our bucket list, we stayed in Port Douglas for another day before returning our rental car to Cairns. We planned to catch a bus to our next destination – Townsville – Far North Queensland's unofficial capital, despite what Cairns' residents would have you believe.

The bus left Cairns at noon and we settled in for the seven-hour drive. There were just a handful of passengers onboard, backpackers mostly, no doubt heading for the party scene on the Gold Coast. On our way south, we passed through some of the wettest places in the country – towns where the annual rainfall is measured in metres, not centimetres. Each year they competed for the most rain, with a peculiar prize up for grabs – a golden gumboot. While other parts of the country sweltered through endless drought, Far North Queensland frequently received drenchings of Biblical proportions. Many locals question whether this part of Queensland deserves the title of the 'Sunshine State'.

The heaviest rainfall on record occurred in 1950 when the town of Tully, 140 kilometres south of Cairns, received a whopping 7.93 metres of rainfall, enough to drown even the tallest giraffe, if there were any in town at the time. As one local put it, 'That particular year, the animals were walking around hand-in-hand looking for a boat.'

We drove past Innisfail, Silkwood and the famous Mission Beach – a popular tourist spot that caters both to families and those looking for a romantic getaway – before stopping at Cardwell, a sleepy coastal town that marks the midway point between Cairns and Townsville. As we got off the bus for a toilet break and a coffee at the café, an enormous orange crab with giant claws and robotic black eyes loomed over us menacingly. The crustacean was our introduction to Australia's strange fixation with 'big things'.

No one knows how or why the fixation developed, however, most people cite the eleven-metre-long 'Big Banana', which popped up one morning in Coffs Harbour in New South Wales in 1964, as the originator. Since then there's been a profusion of monster constructions right across Australia. There's the Big Lobster in Kingston, South Australia. The Big Merino in Goulburn, New South Wales. The Big Pineapple in Woombye, Queensland. And the Big Koala in Cowes, Victoria. Apparently, there's even a five-metre 'Big Poo' in a town called Kiama, which was built as an act of political protest. Though I suspect this is an urban myth.

'Welcome to tropical paradise!' said Drake, our soft-spoken and ever-smiling guesthouse proprietor as we got into Townsville that evening. Drake and his daughter Eva managed the Civic Guesthouse which was located in a quiet downtown side street just a few minutes' walk from Flinders Mall. It was also within walking distance of the Strand – a three-kilometre-long landscaped promenade that overlooks the Coral Sea and provides access to Townsville's beaches and parks.

Unable to find any Airbnb accommodation, we'd booked into the Civic for a couple of nights and were lucky to nab an en suite room for the price of a shared-facility double. Drake, in his trademark friendly manner, showed us around. The guesthouse had a good reputation with overseas backpackers; the French outnumbered most other nationalities, but there were travellers from Israel, Greece, America and New Zealand, to name just a few.

A communal kitchen at the rear of the hostel was clean, functional and well laid out. This opened into a tiled room which served as a rest-cum-gaming area, with a gleaming new pool table taking centre stage. The courtyard and the communal areas had low-set sofas, and plenty of chairs and tables – perfect for socialising, with some of the liveliest experiences occurring in the common areas.

After a quick shower and a change of clothes, we headed out for our budget foot-long Subway sandwich. We then checked out Flinders Street which was abuzz with activity, with smartly dressed locals enjoying dinner at the waterfront cafés and restaurants. At the same time, a younger crowd was headed towards the northern end of the street with its pubs and bars, drawn to the rhythmic beats.

We bought some groceries so that we could make our own meals. Ambika was slightly worried about leaving our food in the communal fridges, but I convinced her that it would be safe – just as long as we labelled everything. Who would take stuff clearly belonging to someone else?

The next morning I went for a run, and when I came back I knew immediately something was up. A glum-looking Ambika was sitting in the far corner of the dining area, alone, watching the other backpackers intently. By now, I had developed that essential skill of intuitively knowing when your spouse is furious. When I asked her what was wrong, she stormed over to the fridge and unceremoniously pulled out an empty two-litre milk bottle labelled 'Rebello' in big, bold letters. Ambika looked at me as if to say 'I told you so' then went and plonked herself back at the dining table and continued her surveillance.

I may only have been recently married, but I was a quick learner, and I knew that there were moments when one's spouse must be left alone. This was one of those occasions. I waited a few minutes, then quietly pulled up a chair and sat down beside her and joined her in her mission to spot the culprit. I must admit, I was at a loss, however, at how we would achieve this. Was Ambika looking for someone with a water bottle filled with milk slinking away in the shadows? Or maybe a tell-tale 'milk moustache' on the offender's lips? Or perhaps she expected the guilty party to crumble under her intense gaze and admit the crime. Whatever the case, I was too afraid to ask and chose to stay silent, lest I become the focus of her wrath.

Once the mood had improved – but sadly with no culprit caught – I suggested a walk along the Strand. After our breakfast of eggs and bread – *sans* milk – we left the hostel and in no time at all were on the south-eastern side of Townsville's main promenade. While not quite as popular with overseas visitors as some of its neighbours, Townsville does well out of domestic tourists and intrepid backpackers and has plenty to offer. Boasting over three hundred days of sunshine a year and a laid-back, tropical atmosphere, it's the kind of place you visit when you want to wind down.

It was yet another glorious day with clear blue skies and a gentle breeze carrying the scents of frangipani and orchid. It felt as if we were walking through one glorious postcard after another, each vista showing happy locals delighting in different activities. Cyclists and joggers zipped past; young families with kids were having a splendid time at the splash park; and beach revellers basked on the sands while others swam in the warm, placid waters of the bay. People picnicked in the park, and the delicious aromas of sizzling sausages and caramelised onions made our mouths water.

Across the bay, just a short ferry ride away, lay Magnetic Island, fondly called 'Maggie' by the locals. It got its name because of the apparent 'magnetic' effect it had on the *Endeavour*'s compass when Captain Cook sailed by. With its sheltered coves, camping grounds, parks and miles of virgin sands, the island was a classic gateway island for locals and visitors alike.

Our walk culminated at the western end of the Strand, which was dominated by a big, oval-shaped community pool. A natural saltwater enclosure, the Strand Rockpool offers year-round safe swimming, essential during the dreaded jellyfish season which lasts from December to March. A flight of rough-hewn stairs led up to a lookout known as Kissing Point, where we enjoyed sweeping views of Cleveland Bay and the Coral Sea as well as the headland of Lucinda with faint glimpses of the off-lying Orpheus chain of islands to the far north.

At the nearby Anzac Memorial Park we stopped to admire the war memorials commemorating those who'd fought and lost their lives over the years. For a young country with no physical borders and no real enemies, Australians had a rich war history, with many battles fought overseas on behalf of the Commonwealth.

The Kissing Point lookout and adjacent land (which houses the old Jezzine Barracks) is a significant military site and marks the location of the original fortifications established in 1891 after the British withdrew from the colonies. Home to the 31st Battalion for over one hundred and twenty years, the beautifully preserved parade grounds and quadrangles, the weathered mounting block and machine-gun mountings, the century-old explosives store, and the imposing turrets, tell a compelling story of valour on foreign soil, of selfless sacrifice on a grand scale and of indomitable courage in the face of danger.

During World War I when Britain went to war with Germany on 4 August 1914, Australia was automatically placed on the side of Great Britain. The first significant Australian action of the war occurred with the Australian Naval and Military Expeditionary Force's (ANMEF) landing in Rabaul on 11 September 1914. Within a week the ANMEF had taken possession of German New Guinea and in October was to take control of the neighbouring islands of the Bismarck Archipelago. On 9 November 1914 the Royal Australian Navy made a major contribution when HMAS *Sydney* destroyed the German raider SMS *Emden*.

In 1915, Australian and New Zealand soldiers formed a part of the expedition that set out to secure Turkey's Gallipoli Peninsula in order to open the Dardanelles to the Allied navies. The ultimate objective was to capture Constantinople (now Istanbul), the capital of the Turkish Ottoman Empire, a staunch ally of Germany. The Australian and New Zealand forces landed at Gallipoli on 25 April, meeting fierce resistance. The British and French soldiers also formed a part of this invasion, landing at Cape Helles on the southern tip of Gallipoli, about 30 kilometres south of the ANZAC landing spot. What was planned as a bold strike to knock Turkey out of the war quickly became a stalemate which dragged on for eight long months. At the end of 1915, the Allied forces were evacuated from the peninsula, with both sides having suffered heavy casualties and endured great hardships. More than 8000 Australian soldiers died in the campaign.

Gallipoli had a profound impact on Australians at home. Today, 25 April is known as ANZAC (Australian and New Zealand Army Corps) Day, a day of national remembrance. Commemorative services are held across the nation at dawn – the precise time of the Gallipoli landing. Although the campaign failed in its military objectives, the actions of Australian and New Zealand forces left a powerful legacy. The 'Anzac legend' became an essential part of the identity of both nations, shaping how they view their past and future.

India too faced a similar dilemma when World War I erupted. As it was considered a part of the British Empire, Indian soldiers entered the battle shoulder to shoulder with British troops. Those with influence within India, including the Indian National Congress, believed that the cause of Indian independence would best be served by helping Britain, and offers of financial and military assistance were made from all over the country. Even some of the wealthy princes pledged vast sums of money for the cause. Indian forces were ready for battle before most other soldiers in the Dominions, the first Indian troops arriving on the Western Front by the winter of 1914 and fighting at Ypres in Belgium.

According to one war statistic, over one million Indian troops served overseas during World War I, suffering some 60,000 casualties, a number similar to their Australian counterparts. In fact, nearly 15,000 Indian soldiers fought side by side Australians and New Zealanders at Gallipoli of which 1400 died and 3500 ended up wounded, a fact sadly forgotten by many. Photographs and sketches from the time show Indian and Australian soldiers on and off the field of war. Australians were first introduced to the Indian staple diet of daal and rotis on dusty foreign battlefields, and the professionalism of the Indian soldiers quickly cemented their friendship.

There are countless Australian and New Zealand accounts – from soldiers' diaries or in photographs – where they refer to 'my Indian friend' or 'my Gurkha friend'.

Of all the British Empire's colonies, India contributed the most men to the war effort – around 1.5 million. Self-governing nations within the Empire, including Canada, South Africa, Australia, New Zealand and Newfoundland, contributed a further 1.3 million. Although rarely acknowledged, more Indians fought with and for the British from 1914 to 1918 than the combined total of Canadian, South African, Australian and New Zealand, troops.

The Gallipoli campaign was one of the first international events that saw Australians taking part in a global war. The event forged a sense of national identity for the new country. On the world stage, Australian soldiers epitomised traits of endurance, ingenuity, larrikinism, egalitarianism and mateship. For Australia, World War I remains the costliest conflict in terms of deaths and casualties. From a population of fewer than five million, 416,809 men enlisted and fought in numerous campaigns, with more than 60,000 eventually killed and 156,000 wounded, gassed, or taken prisoner.

But the horrors of war returned to haunt the world within two decades when World War II erupted. The third of September 1939 was the beginning of Australia's involvement in World War II and almost a million Australians, both men and women, enlisted to serve in the armed forces. The soldiers, or 'diggers' as they were referred to, fought in campaigns against Germany and Italy in Europe, the Mediterranean and North Africa, as well as against Japan in South-East Asia and other parts of the Pacific. Australia had always supported Britain during times of conflict, however that changed on 7 December 1941, when Japan bombed Pearl Harbor. Just two months into his new role as Prime Minister, John Curtin's worst fears had come true. Over the next four months, Japan ruthlessly destroyed the myth that Britannia ruled the seas, making a rapid and devastating downward thrust into South-East Asia. Singapore, Britain's most extensive naval base in this region collapsed. Malaya, Indonesia and Timor soon succumbed, followed by the decimation of Australian-administered Rabaul in New Guinea. The Japanese victory which had seemed like a distant possibility was quickly turning into a terrifying reality. War was on Australia's doorstep, but there was no one to defend the country.

Curtin had warned the government as far back as 1936 that 'the dependence of Australia upon the competence, let alone the readiness, of British statesmen to send forces to our aid is too dangerous a hazard upon which to found Australia's defence policy'. Winston Churchill had made it clear that, if forced to choose, he would use English troops and equipment to defend England rather than helping to protect Australia against the Japanese in the Pacific.

On 27 December 1941, Curtin published a radical message in the *Melbourne Herald* which signalled a shift in strategic thinking: 'Australia looks to America, free of any pangs as to our traditional links or kinship with the United Kingdom.' To Winston Churchill's dismay and the shock of many older Australians who remained fiercely loyal to England, the country consciously discarded its old allegiance, prioritised its survival, and looked to the USA for help. By mid-1942, Japan had taken Hong Kong. The Philippines soon followed. In almost no time at all, the Imperial Army had reached the shores of New Guinea. Three months after Curtin's New Year's message, US President Roosevelt sent troops to the Pacific and, by 1943, there were some 250,000 Americans stationed in Melbourne, Sydney and Brisbane.

On 19 February 1942, Darwin was hit. War had finally arrived on Australian shores. Japanese fighters and bombers attacked the city twice, killing two hundred and fifty-two allied service personnel and civilians. On 3 March, Broome, in Western Australia, was strafed. In succeeding months air attacks were made on many towns in northern Australia including Wyndham, Port Hedland and Derby in Western Australia, Darwin and Katherine in the Northern Territory, Townsville and Mossman in Queensland, and Horn Island in the Torres Strait. Darwin, in particular, was under constant harassment and faced nearly sixty-four separate attacks by the Japanese air force, the last of these bombings occurring towards the end of 1943.

On 7 May 1945, the German High Command authorised the signing of an unconditional surrender on all fronts. The war in Europe was finally over. And on 14 August, Japan surrendered to the allied forces. Some 39,000 Australian lives had been lost, but Australia itself had been spared the worst of the devastation. The new Prime Minister, Ben Chifley, announced the news of the end of the war in a special radio broadcast at 9.30 a.m. on Wednesday 15 August. Australian cities and towns immediately erupted in spontaneous carnival and celebration.

While it's true that Australia aligned with the USA in 1942, it's untrue – or rather a misleading oversimplification – that Australia 'dumped' Britain. The Australia–USA partnership was a marriage of convenience but Australia's commitment to the Empire remained intact. Australia's hierarchy of priorities had changed; however, it decided to defend itself first before rushing off to protect the Commonwealth or allies overseas. The wars, in a way, matured Australia, and the nation has made its presence felt on the international stage ever since.

CHAPTER 16
Adieu to Queensland

If all difficulties were known at the outset of a long journey, most of us would never start out at all – Dan Rather

Back at the hostel, a different kind of war was brewing. As we made our way to the communal kitchen with a bag full of groceries – including two more litres of milk – we heard a commotion. Somehow or other, the hostel guests had identified an alleged serial thief in our midst. Our milk was just one of the items that had been pilfered. Entering the kitchen, we saw a young French couple and a German backpacker confronting a young Mexican girl who stood with her back to the wall, shaking like a leaf.

In her late twenties, Ilsa had seemed like a decent enough girl when we met her the day before. She was backpacking across Australia just like us and had been here for three months. She planned to stay in Townsville for a few weeks more before heading to Perth in Western Australia. She did seem a bit nervous but we didn't know why. She also seemed to hang around the kitchen at odd hours, opening fridges and rummaging through the pantry. We didn't think much of it.

Just minutes before we arrived back from our walk, the French couple had caught Ilsa going through their lunchbox. It didn't take long for hostilities to break out and pretty soon practically every other guest was involved. A quiet Japanese couple told us that just the day before some of their Asian condiments had mysteriously gone missing. They were understandably angry. Ambika, too, wasted no time in joining the fray, calmly handing me our bag of groceries and joining the advancing allied forces as they bore down on poor Ilsa. The Japanese couple edged closer to get a ringside view.

Ilsa seemed to realise there was no way out and fessed up, apologising profusely to the group in lilting Spanish, 'Lo siento mucho a todas!'. As if on cue, a burly South African guest intervened and with an air of authority put an end to the fight. The advancing forces accepted Ilsa's unconditional surrender and banned her from using the fridge. The battle was over before it even began and the entire guesthouse broke into a round of applause as Ilsa left the kitchen. Even the Japanese couple flashed a smile and hi-fived the victors. Ambika meanwhile got busy dissecting Ilsa's plot with the rest of the group, deciphering the possible motives, figuring out the strategies and gauging the amount of loot she might have pinched. The love of my life had truly warmed up to hostel living.

We'd been on the road for nearly a month by this stage and hadn't fielded a single job interview lead, let alone an offer. Admittedly, we weren't trying our hardest, but the writing seemed to be on the wall. My experience as a ship's captain and Ambika's stellar career in India counted for little here in Australia. And our timing was bad. Unemployment was at its peak in 2014 at just over 6 per cent, and we'd arrived in the middle of a depressed job market where migrants were competing with locals for work.

Unlike migrants from generations past, most new arrivals gravitated towards the major capital cities. Sydney and Melbourne were the prime destinations and were already groaning under the weight of their booming populations. Understandably, many average Australians were angry with the government's immigration policies. Did the country need so many skilled migrants when locals were struggling to find a job? Was the migrant work visa, which allowed companies to hire overseas talent with ease, undermining the chances of future Australians?

As far as I could see, Australia's immigration policies were some of the most stringent in the world. The impetus for bringing in new migrants was driven by a range of factors, one of which was the forecasted long-term economic benefits. But the policy was not easy to sell to someone struggling to put food on the table. There were no quick solutions.

To make matters worse, the shipping industry was in turmoil due to declining oil prices. Only a few commercial ships flying the Australian flag existed, and coastal shipping, or what was left of it, was struggling. Such was the unstable economic environment we found ourselves in. I'd be lucky to find a job at all, let alone one in my chosen industry.

Although we didn't talk about it openly, Ambika and I knew that very soon our carefree wanderings would have to come to an end. We'd then be faced with the daunting prospect of finding a job, most probably on the lowest rungs of our respective professions, and starting all over again. Would Australia be the promised land for us just as it was for so many other migrants? Would we be another success story in the land of plenty? Or would our decision to leave a life of relative comfort and security – an idea that seemed so logical when I envisaged it from 6000 kilometres away – undermine all our achievements to date?

I felt fluttering anxiety begin to grow in the pit of my stomach. A voice inside my head began berating me for inventing such a ludicrous plan. Unbeknown to Ambika, I was waking up in the middle of the night in a cold sweat, my throat dry with fear. I was afraid of the consequences if things didn't work out. The last thing I wanted was to have Ambika follow me down a path of ruin. My only recourse in those moments was faith. Faith and a beautiful quote from Ralph Waldo Emerson which had always held me in good stead in moments of self-doubt: 'There's nothing capricious in nature, and the implanting of a desire indicates that its gratification is in the constitution of the creature that feels it.'

Someone I was keen to meet in Townsville was Frank D'Souza, the Regional Harbour Master for the ports of Townsville, Abbot Point and Lucinda. I got Frank's reference from Glenn Saldanha in Mackay and made contact the day we arrived. I didn't expect to hear back from him and was genuinely surprised when he phoned.

Frank collected us from the hostel, and what was meant to be a quick 'hello' ended up being much more. A man of few words, he drove us to his 'office' at the entrance to the Port of Townsville on the edge of Ross Creek. He showed us around the Vessel Traffic Service command centre, similar to an Air Traffic Control tower at an airport. The command room was modern with five semi-circular consoles equally spaced around the rectangular, windowless room. One wall was covered with giant, high-definition LCD screens where a diverse range of maps, environmental data and ship information was projected real-time. The command centre controlled and managed all shipping across the entire Great Barrier Reef area – a mammoth effort that oversaw 2300 kilometres of coastline from Bundaberg in the south to the Torres Strait in the north.

That evening, Frank invited us to a friend's party. The fact that we didn't know anyone – and had only just met Frank – didn't seem to matter. Pria, Frank's wife, seemed genuinely happy to meet us and wanted to know all about our backpacking adventures. She worked at one of the Catholic schools in town and did philanthropic and community work in her spare time. On the way to the party, she told us about her and Frank's migration journey and the struggles they'd faced when they arrived in Australia more than a decade ago. A fellow mariner, Frank had had a lot of trouble finding a job but with determination and the help and support of friends and other migrants they succeeded. Now they were living the Australian dream in a beautiful house with a swimming pool; they had a nice car and an altogether enviable lifestyle.

The party's host was a sprightly man named Rowland who must have been in his eighties but had the bounce and vigour of a twenty-year-old. His guests, without exception, were all migrants who had arrived in Australia decades ago. Their children were now first-generation Australians. It was an evening filled with lively conversation that ranged across domestic politics, the state of affairs back in India, the weather in Queensland, the performance of the Australian cricket team, and everyone's travel plans for the next holidays. The warmth of the people around the table, the general banter amongst long-time friends and the simple joy of enjoying home-cooked food was a memorable experience for us.

Of all the other stories I heard that night, it was Rowland's story that I found the most inspiring. Half-German and half-Singaporean by descent, Rowland was a young boy in an orphanage in Singapore under the custody of Canossian nuns when the Imperial Japanese Army invaded in 1942. The Japanese forced six of the nuns and one hundred and forty-eight children to leave and banished them to the Bahau jungle in Malaya. The nuns and their charges stayed there for nearly three years, surviving on frogs, berries and snails. There were no medical facilities, and tropical diseases were rampant. Many children contracted malaria, dysentery and beriberi and died; some others were attacked by wild animals.

The survivors who made it back to civilisation at the end of the war bore scars that would never fade. Rowland eventually married the niece of a Kesseler priest, migrated to Australia and enlisted in the Australian military as soon as he became a naturalised citizen. He was hardened by his experiences as a child and his time in the army. He had recently lost his wife to cancer and lived by himself, but his resilient spirit seldom allowed him to wallow in self-pity. He was always keen to make new friends and took us under his wing, even teaching us how to play Mahjong, the Chinese game of skill and strategy.

That night I dreamt of dusty battlefields, swooping enemy planes, children playing Chinese checkers and strangers offering me watery daal and stiff, dust-caked rotis in dugout trenches.

Townsville marked our last stop in Queensland. We were headed next for Victoria in the far south, the oldest and (pardon me for saying this, Queenslanders!) most sophisticated Australian state. Although just one-tenth the size of Queensland, Victoria promised spectacular scenery with sweeping coastlines, pristine beaches, world-class wine regions, and so much more. The state also hosted some of Australia's premier sporting and cultural events and had a rich colonial and Indigenous history. We booked a late evening flight to Melbourne and were due to fly out in two days.

Of all the places we'd visited, Townsville was the one town that we explored the least. But it was also the place where we forged some of our greatest friendships. For our final night we booked a room in an Airbnb townhouse, more so because of the glowing review than the facilities. Trisha, our host, kindly offered to pick us up from the hostel. As we waited with our sagging backpacks and faithful wheelie bag, we heard rather than saw her old grey Peugeot 306 rattling down the road.

In her early twenties, Trisha had migrated from Bangalore in India in search of better prospects. Australia was one of her preferred choices, the others being the UK and Canada. In the end Australia won. She fell in love with the laid-back lifestyle and the myriad of career opportunities and decided to stay. She was now a naturalised Australian citizen completing her Masters in Political Science while working part-time at a local café. She had also recently married. Her husband, Jonathan, was an Australian whose father had been part of the 'Ten Pound Pom' scheme. Jonathan hailed from Alstonville, a sleepy village set among the fertile rolling hills a short distance from Byron Bay, the surfing capital of New South Wales.

The couple lived in a two-storey townhouse in a quiet suburb a few kilometres from the city centre. The bedrooms were located on the upper level while the downstairs level had an open-plan kitchen, dining area and lounge room. The Airbnb website had described Trisha as a 'tea aficionado' and a person who 'loved to make new friends'. Jonathan, who joined us later that evening, turned out to be a gentle, soft-spoken guy who was working as a graduate architect. He told us he came from a modern Christian family and was one of four siblings. By his own account, he had one of the best upbringings anyone could have wished for. The couple met at a community lunch organised at an inner-city church in Brisbane for homeless people, immigrants and international students. They would both occasionally do volunteer work there, and during the weekly planning meetings, their love blossomed.

Trisha hailed from Southern India where caste, socio-economic background and religious affiliations were critical when it came to marriage. Prior approval from parents was usually a prerequisite. Weddings were a strictly regulated affair, and a proposal usually involved a full background check, a rigorous dissection of the family tree and a series of council meetings. Luckily for Trisha, her parents were anything but traditional and had been living in Australia for some time when Jonathan proposed. His gentle nature and respect for elders and women won the hearts of Trisha's parents and they gave their blessing without reservation.

Jonathan loved India and felt a deep sense of connection with the land that echoed Trisha's links with the country. The couple had made a few trips back to India and Trisha told us of her husband's love of crispy dosas; his attempts at wearing the traditional dhotis; and his fascination with the Indian public transport system – overcrowded buses, cacophonous auto-rickshaws and 'characterful' railways!

Their relaxed lifestyle and love for simple things, as well as their daily struggles and small joys, provided us with an invaluable insight into life in Australia. We stayed with them for just one night, but by the time we left, it felt like we had known them forever. On the day we were due to fly out, they accompanied us to the airport and bid us a fond farewell. We promised we'd stay in touch.

The flight to Melbourne marked our exit from Queensland, a state which we'd discovered to be a vast land of immense and diverse natural beauty. Its people were down-to-earth and easy-going with a self-deprecating humour and an unpretentious attitude. Knowingly or unknowingly, unfairly or not, we would henceforth benchmark everywhere else we visited against the magnificent 'Sunshine State'.

CHAPTER 17
The Gold Rush

Be fearless in the pursuit of what sets your soul on fire
– Jennifer Lee

'Beware of her charming ways, and her wild mood swings,' a friend told me when we said we were visiting Melbourne. Like most Melburnians, he was smitten by the enchanting beauty of his hometown and considered the unpredictable weather that caught many visitors off guard just a trifling inconvenience.

Consistently ranked as one of the most 'liveable' cities in the world, Melbourne scores well when it comes to education, entertainment, health care, research and development, not to mention tourism, sport, eating and drinking! But this stellar performance is no recent occurrence: the city has been a trailblazer ever since John Batman selected a site on the banks of the Yarra as an ideal spot for a 'village' back in 1835.

Things took off in the 1850s with the discovery of vast quantities of gold in the central part of the state (around what is today Bendigo and Ballarat). Take the case of Cornish miner John Deason, just one of the countless success stories. On 5 February 1869, Deason and his prospecting partner Richard Oates found a large nugget just a few centimetres below the surface near the town of Moliagul. Aware of the stiff competition from fellow prospectors and the security risks of carrying around a large amount of gold, they decided to wait until nightfall before digging it out of the ground. Under cover of darkness and barely able to contain their excitement, they took it to the bank in the nearby township of Dunolly, where the next morning it had to be broken in half before it would fit on the scales. The nugget weighed a jaw-dropping 70 kilograms (around 2300 ounces), and Deason and Oates received a staggering £9381 (more than $5 million today).

'Gold fever' swiftly engulfed the nation. From across the country and around the world, farmers, shepherds, labourers, schoolteachers and people from all walks of life flocked to the region with nothing but a shovel, a pickaxe and lofty dreams of getting rich overnight. They did not have to look very far or try very hard back in those early days. In some areas, gold could be found beneath a thin layer of topsoil. A few hours' lucky digging might mean never having to work again.

In 1854, the Victorian Gold Discovery Committee proclaimed: 'The discovery of (gold) has converted a remote dependency into a country of world-wide fame; it has attracted a population, extraordinary in number, with unprecedented rapidity; it has enhanced the value of property to an enormous extent; it has made this the richest country in the world; and, in less than three years, it has done for this colony the work of an age, and made its impulses felt in the most distant regions of the earth.'

According to state records, Victoria accounted for more than a third of the world's total gold output in the 1850s. At its peak, some *two tonnes* of gold per week flowed into the Treasury in Melbourne. It's claimed that the gold exported to Britain during that period paid all her foreign debts and helped lay the foundation of her enormous commercial expansion in the latter half of the century.

In less than a decade, Melbourne went from being a distant colonial town on the fringes of civilisation to a booming metropolis with the beaming confidence and gait of a prized racehorse. Suddenly Australia was the preferred trading partner for the major economies of the time. The wealth generated sparked record imports while the towns at the centre of the boom enjoyed substantial business investment and demand for local produce.

Remarkably, the gold rush story is still far from over, and Australia remains the world's second-largest gold producer. It gives me the shudders just imagining who the next person may be to accidentally stumble upon a priceless nugget somewhere in the uncharted expanse of the outback.

Back in the 1850s Victoria, the gold rush brought some unique challenges, which subsequently shaped the identity of this emerging nation. In some towns where a lot of gold was found, populations frequently grew by over 1000 per cent. Rutherglen in north-eastern Victoria, for example, went from 2000 to nearly 60,000 residents in less than ten years! The pressure this sort of expansion must have put on infrastructures such as housing, transport and other facilities is almost unimaginable.

The camaraderie and 'mateship' that developed on the goldfields is to this day integral to how the locals – and the rest of the world – perceive Australians. The diggers' defiance and open disdain of authority remain a theme in any discussion of Australia's history and national identity. Australia's World War I 'diggers' (named after their goldfield predecessors) at Gallipoli for example are reverently remembered as mates in the trenches who had a healthy disrespect for their 'English superiors'. The gold rush also laid the seeds for multiculturalism. The majority of prospectors were British, but there were American, French, Italian, German, Polish, Hungarian and Chinese as well.

With so much money splashing around, a program of grand civic construction in Victoria's capital city soon began. The 'boom period' of the 1850s and 1860s saw the construction of Victoria's Parliament House, the Treasury Building, the State Library, the University of Melbourne, the General Post Office, Customs House, the Melbourne Town Hall, and St Patrick's Cathedral, to name just a few. Much of what we see today in the city centre is testimony to Melbourne's imperial status. Even after the gold rush ended, Melbourne continued to grow as it diversified into agricultural exports and manufacturing. During the 1880s, for a brief time, it was the wealthiest city in the world and the largest after London in the British Empire. Not bad for a rural outpost in the far corner of the world, yet to be reborn as a new country.

The Gold Rush

With such a rich and fascinating history, how could I not fall in love with the place? As our plane began its descent, the city lights sparkled below us like a million little stars. We could make out beautifully landscaped gardens and a profusion of parks. Large open spaces, giant stadiums and sports arenas were lit up with high-intensity floodlights, while the inky black Yarra River meandered its merry course through it all.

We were picked up at the airport by Harsha, a friend of a friend of mine in India. Although we'd never met, Harsha offered to have us stay for a couple of nights at his home in Kensington, in inner-city Melbourne, which was lucky, as we were unable to find any suitable accommodation as Melbourne was gripped with Australian Football League (AFL) fever. An IT professional with a passion for music, Harsha certainly looked the part with his bushy Rastafarian beard, a perpetual sparkle in his eye and a cheeky grin that spoke volumes about his warm nature and his wild spirit. My Couchsurfing friend Satya described Harsha as, 'a musician at heart, an adventurer, a great cook, a foodie, a fitness enthusiast, a biker and a handsome jolly good fellow with a suave charm and a million friends.' We bonded instantly. As we zipped through the suburbs, he regaled us with stories of Melbourne while pointing out key landmarks. In the half-hour drive to his home, we realised one thing: to see everything this city had to offer we were going to need more time.

Harsha and his wife Pavitra lived in a cosy two-bedroom unit in a modern high-rise with sweeping views of the Maribyrnong River, the famous Flemington Racecourse (which hosts the iconic Melbourne Cup – the race that 'stops the nation') and the city skyline. The second bedroom doubled as an in-house studio and was crammed with a drum kit, keyboards, electric guitars and an array of sound recording and DJ equipment. We slept soundly that night with a cymbal at our feet and a gleaming trumpet near our headboard, a fitting backdrop for our first night in Melbourne, a city that proudly took the lead over other Australian cities in the field of fine arts.

We woke the next morning to an empty flat, a well-stocked pantry, and a wintry crispness in the air – a welcome relief after a month in the tropics. We planned to spend the day organising the Victorian leg of our trip and, if we had time, investigating what we'd do in Canberra and Sydney as well. But just then, my phone rang shrilly. It was an HR manager for an offshore shipping company based in Western Australia. It turned out they were looking for a navigation officer to join a supply ship that serviced the oil fields in the country's far north-west. The HR manager had received the resumé I'd sent while we were in Brisbane. This was fantastic news, although the timing could have been better. The company needed someone for an eight-week contract – starting the very next day – and so the discussion quickly turned to verifying my certificates and other logistics.

This was a surprise development, but Ambika took the news in her stride and suggested she could fly to Brisbane and stay in rental accommodation if I got the job. The one thing we knew by then was that as migrants seeking employment in a new country you never turned down an offer. Ever. I had to say yes.

While in the throes of packing our bags and cancelling our forward bookings, the HR manager rang back. Due to a change in the vessel's itinerary, the ship was now departing overseas – with the same crew. He was very sorry, but I didn't have the job, after all. I felt simultaneously elated and deflated. But I chose to see it as a positive development: the door to securing employment in Australia had just opened a little bit wider. It also meant that we could continue with our travels as planned!

That afternoon, we hopped on a tram and headed into the city. After St Petersburg, Berlin and Vienna, Melbourne's century-old tram network is the fourth largest in the world and still retains its heritage charm. What began as a pathway for horse-drawn vehicles in 1884 evolved into an efficient mode of transport which ferries over 200 million passengers every year.

We alighted in the city centre and found ourselves caught in the middle of the evening rush hour. Melbourne seemed to heave and sigh with a tired yet patient rhythm: alternating between nostalgic contemplation of its past achievements and grand visions of future growth. We didn't venture far from Flinders Street Station, and were happy to sit for a while in the Federation Square forecourt and watch the city go about its business. Fed Square's stern, deconstructionist style, where angular, cranked geometric shapes form a rather modern and abstract design, certainly mark it out among the adjoining colonial buildings.

Harsha picked us up after he finished work and took us to meet some friends at an Indian restaurant in the outer suburb of Dandenong. On the way, we witnessed our first torrential and unannounced downpour. Harsha was unfazed and told us Melburnians were accustomed to having 'four seasons in one day'. Most carried a sun hat, an umbrella and a winter jacket – whatever the time of the year.

He played us some songs that he'd compiled in the very room that we'd slept in the night before. A retro fusion of Indian and electronica, The Fifths, as his band was called, created snappy, upbeat music which had a unique new-age Indianness interwoven into it. His fellow band members all worked full-time and met up on the weekends to practise. Harsha migrated to Australia partly to pursue his music, which he said was harder to do back in India. His band was working towards launching an EP soon and were performing live at various venues across Melbourne.

The Dosa Plaza was a clear favourite with the local Indian community. In between savouring twelve-dollar dosas and gulping down six-dollar aloo-chaats (expensive compared to what we were used to paying in India) we met a second-generation Australian–Indian urologist named Ranjit and his wife Kanchana who practised holistic therapies. Another Indian couple we met owned and operated a Bollywood dance studio, as this dance form was a big thing in Melbourne. I have to admit meeting fellow Indians who were already settled and living a life of comfort and security was confronting. For a second, I wondered if Ambika and I should have started looking for work as soon as we arrived. But the group unanimously praised our courage for doing something bold and gave us plenty of encouragement, wishing us well on our journey.

On the drive home, Harsha told us he'd moved to Australia in 2001 to study business at university. After finishing his degree, he worked for a few years, then went back to India, got married but decided to return to Melbourne in 2010, this time for good. When I asked him what his first impressions of the country were, he replied matter-of-factly, 'My first impression that still remains to this day is the feeling of freedom from being judged. It was a challenging time as I had to shed my reservations about living as a migrant and learn many life lessons. It was a steep learning curve, but I picked up all the required skills I'd need to live as a student, to work, and integrate with locals and contribute meaningfully to the community. I was establishing new friendships but it took time and effort. In the end, it was all worth it!'

His advice was to take it slow and easy during the initial settling-in phase. He assured us that although it'd be tough in the beginning, eventually we'd achieve a comfortable lifestyle and would be in a position to chase our dreams, however distant they might seem.

The next morning, as we got ready to move to our Airbnb accommodation, we met Harsha's wife Pavitra. A vibrant and cheerful person, Pavi was studying Korean at weekend school while working full-time as an account manager for an insurance company. She planned to travel to South Korea towards the end of her studies as part of a Victorian Government scholarship exchange program. For me, this was one of the biggest drawcards about living in Australia – the ability to pursue any career path, to chase any dream, and to be able to do so at any stage of life.

CHAPTER 18

The Grand Dame

All you need to know is that it's possible – Wolf, an Appalachian Trail Hiker

On their way to work the next day, Harsha and Pavitra kindly dropped us off at our Airbnb accommodation. Rebecca's single-storey Victorian weatherboard house sat in a neat row of adjoining houses in a quiet side street in Footscray, a charming inner-western suburb of Melbourne. The house's cream-coloured exterior reflected the morning light while the pitched roof and slender brick chimney gave the building a rustic feel. A big mullioned window with frosted windows overlooked a small front yard overrun with a profusion of natural shrubs. Clusters of beautiful daffodils reared their golden heads at the entrance to the property, adding just the right amount of colour.

Bec and her two rumbustious dogs greeted us warmly at the doorstep. Ditto was a plump Staffie, while Ditty was part Jack Russell, part Border collie and many parts unknown, fondly referred to as 'Heinz 57'. A fifth-generation Australian, her ancestors arrived during the gold rush. She was a warm and accommodating hostess, and we spent some time getting to know each other over a cup of tea.

Rebecca's home was like a quaint English country house in the rolling hills of rural England: all polished wooden floorboards; a brick fireplace in the living room; and French doors leading to a quaint rear courtyard. I could picture Bec hosting a tea party on a lazy afternoon with warm buttered scones and Earl Grey tea served in delicate chinaware. Our bedroom off the central hallway was stacked from floor to ceiling with rows of books, meticulously arranged according to the genre. A robust timber table, a couch, a full-length mirror and a queen-sized bed with fresh cotton sheets gave it a homely feel. But Melbourne had a lot to offer, and we were running out of time, so we unpacked, freshened up, and headed straight into the city by train.

Melbourne unfolds like a realist landscape painting stretching linearly from its rich colonial past into its exciting yet uncertain future. It does what most other cities fail to do, blending antiquity and modernism with a natural and dramatic flair – not layer upon layer where the past gets irretrievably buried – but like a long unravelling and rich tapestry with pleasing contradictions that spanned centuries. It is a city that fearlessly rushes forward, yet at the same time manages to respect its past glories. It promotes art, culture and sport like no other Australian city – from basement rock gigs, to open-air plays, fringe festivals, street art and blockbuster sporting events – there's truly something for everyone.

The city is easy to navigate with many attractions located on a grid of streets within a small radius of Flinders Street Station and the iconic Federation Square. The free trams within the city centre are a great idea, particularly the 'City Circle' heritage tram decorated in distinctive maroon and green with yellow and gold trimmings which runs a circular route between Flinders and La Trobe Streets, all the way down to Docklands and up to Spring Street. Onboard, you get to see landmarks such as the Immigration Museum and the modern Sea Life Aquarium. Across the Yarra, you'll catch a glimpse of the Crown Casino towers, the glass facades of the futuristic skyscrapers unapologetically piercing the blue skies. The tram trundles along La Trobe Street passing the Flagstaff Gardens, the Mint, the magnificent Carlton Gardens, the grand colonnaded Parliament House and the Princess Theatre, both on Spring Street, and the leafy Treasury Gardens. The loop serves as a perfect snapshot for visitors, showcasing the flamboyant vision of the forefathers and the wealth that made it a reality. We found it astounding that most of Melbourne's grand colonial buildings were designed and built at the time when Australia was little more than a fledgling outpost, albeit a cash-rich one thanks to the flourishing gold trade.

Later that afternoon, we visited the southern beachside suburb of St Kilda, a short fifteen-minute tram ride away. A glitzy resort during the Victorian era, St Kilda evolved into a rich man's enclave with palatial mansions and grand terraces cropping up along the foreshore. As we walked along the esplanade, we were captivated by the colourful buildings which retain the charm of a bygone era. Today, most of these large houses have been converted to guesthouses, and their gardens have made way for apartments.

The streets of St Kilda are dotted with characterful cafés, romantic wine bars, fine-dining restaurants and a few old European cakeshops. One of the most prominent landmarks on the beachfront is the century-old Luna Park, Australia's longest-running amusement park, which opened in 1912. You enter through the imposing yet friendly thirty-foot-wide face of Mr Moon, with his toothy grin, arched eyebrows and lively blue eyes wedged in between equally impressive eighty-foot towers. While small compared to other amusement parks around the world, the historic park nevertheless offers tourist and locals alike a nostalgic afternoon of fun.

On the beachfront adjacent to the adjoining and equally imposing Palais Theatre, families were enjoying picnic lunches on beach mats; there were dads playing ball with their kids; people riding bikes and jogging in their spandex; couples holding hands and sharing romantic moments, and youngsters on tricycles with their parents in tow. As the sun descended over the shimmering waters of Port Phillip Bay, we sat on the long timber jetty and took it all in. Although our lives were in a state of happy limbo, I could feel the tide slowly turning in our favour; the goals that we'd dreamt of slowly coming within arm's reach. I couldn't help but feel grateful for this fresh lease of life in such a harmonious and accommodating country.

On Saturday afternoon on the week of our arrival in the city, Harsha invited us to watch the Australian Rules Football (AFL) Grand Final at a friend's house in the leafy, upmarket suburb of Strathmore. The game was being held at the MCG and local heroes Hawthorn were taking on the Sydney Swans. Harsha gave us directions and told us to meet him there. All we knew of Harsha's friend was that his name was Andrew, he was Indian, an ex-captain on commercial ships like me and currently worked at the Port of Melbourne.

When we arrived, Harsha was nowhere to be seen. I called him and he told me he couldn't make it but that we should just go on in and introduce ourselves. Although we felt uncomfortable, what was the worst that could happen? Andrew might slam the door shut in our face thinking we were a couple of freeloaders desperate to watch the footy final and have a free meal. Not the end of the world. I steeled myself and knocked on the front door. Out of her comfort zone and feeling quite mortified, Ambika hid behind me. Andrew opened the door and after a quick introduction and just a moment's hesitation, welcomed us with a big hug.

'If you're Harsha's friends, that's good enough for me!' he said. 'Now, where the hell is he?'

'Harsha couldn't make it and asked me to apologise on his behalf,' I said.

'Oh well, he's going to miss out on my famous chowder!'

Andrew ushered us inside, grabbing the wine bottle we'd brought in one hand and Ambika in the other. Clean-shaven and handsomely bald, he was like a Zen monk and looked much younger than his years.

Andrew's house was spacious and tastefully decorated with plenty of bedrooms, a modern island kitchen, a basement that had been converted into a children's play area and rumpus room, and a beautifully landscaped garden with unhindered views of the Moonee Ponds Creek Reserve and the sprawling suburbs beyond.

His wife Michelle was of Argentinian descent and was busy preparing homemade pizzas and a Caesar salad in the kitchen. The couple met in India in 1997 when Michelle was on holiday with friends. Andrew was a merchant navy officer at the time. A short courtship across the Atlantic ensued, and they married in 2000. They initially moved to Argentina and tried to establish themselves there, but the economic turmoil made life difficult, and the couple decided to migrate to Australia. They were in their late twenties, had no children at that stage and nothing to lose.

Andrew told us those early years were challenging – he was a qualified ship's captain, like me, but the only job he could get was as a telemarketer earning ten dollars an hour. A skilled mariner, Andrew worked ten-hour days and was often bossed around by his manager – a young business graduate fresh out of college with no industry experience whatsoever. Life was difficult and the going was tough. At one point, the couple had just $350 in the bank. Michelle thought about asking her parents for help, but Andrew pleaded with her for one more week's grace. On the last day of that week, after having exhausted all leads, he landed a job as a marine surveyor at the Port of Melbourne. Andrew considered that event to be the turning point in their migration journey.

As the couple had children in quick succession, Michelle chose to be a stay-at-home mum but was socially active. She was into holistic healing therapies and was a certified Reiki healer. In his spare time, Andrew pursued his passion for scuba diving and occasionally travelled to remote and exotic dive sites around the world. His children shared his love for diving and joined him sometimes. Ambika and I listened transfixed.

'Hopefully, we've motivated you to stay committed to this path and to keep applying for jobs until the first break comes along,' Andrew said. 'That's all you need to focus on. Everything will fall in place in time.'

Just then, Ranjit and Kanchana, whom we'd met briefly at the Dosa Plaza a few nights earlier, arrived. They were good friends of Andrew and Michelle's and were pleasantly surprised to see us again.

The couple lived in the inner suburb of Kew with their two kids. Ranjit was a practising surgeon, who was also passionate about golf, yoga and was partial to a nice drop of red wine! He came from a family of doctors and philanthropists and his father, who'd migrated to Australia in the 1960s, worked as a general surgeon and Consul General in Melbourne for twenty-five years. Ranjit was driven by a passion for promoting health and wellness, combining his traditional 'Western' practice with yoga, meditation, nutrition and exercise. But the one passion which overshadowed everything else was his love of golf. He had a handicap of six and was working hard on bringing it down to a four. Kanchana shared Ranjit's interests and practised as a yoga teacher. She also managed Ranjit's surgical business, on top of her busy role as a mother. To us, they seemed like the perfect role models of successful Indian migrants who were Australian in every sense but still followed the ancient traditions and culture of their homeland.

With just minutes until kick-off, we settled in to watch the game, beers in hand. The entire AFL concept was new to me, an Indian migrant who belonged to a cricket-crazy nation, a game played with passion and fervour on every street corner and in every suburb in India. The only contact sport Indians play in an international arena is hockey, so you can imagine my amazement when the Grand Final began and the players started pushing and shoving each other while trying to score a goal with an egg-shaped ball. To the uninitiated, it looked like there was a fully-fledged fight taking place. In broad daylight. And with people cheering every time the stocky men tangled and fell in a heap! Behaviour that could get you in trouble with the law outside the playground, I imagined. Ranjit, a big AFL fan, patiently talked me through the rules of the game, and although I tried my best to follow, I must admit it was all rather confusing.

Ambika and I had just arrived from Queensland, a state which was devoted to NRL (National Rugby League) – the opposing football code, although the treatment meted to players on the field seemed similar in both games. And then there was Rugby Union and Association Football as well. I was beginning to doubt my ability to understand the nuances of this national sport. Melbourne had an NRL team – the Melbourne Storm – but the popularity of the code paled in comparison to the AFL.

Many Victorians didn't even acknowledge NRL as a real sport! I'm sure the Queenslanders had a contradictory opinion. All other states and territories, as far as I could tell, had no say in the matter and ended up playing one of the variations of the game.

Luckily for us, we were still marked as 'stateless' – ergo 'harmless' drifters – and so had the liberty of following both codes, without being judged too harshly. One thing was sure: we could not have picked a better introduction to AFL. The MCG crowd that afternoon neared 100,000 and, in the end, Hawthorn won convincingly. Halfway through, I realised that I just might have found my Australian sport.

Although we enjoyed staying at Rebecca's house, we were spending an hour each day getting into town and back, which was chewing through our sightseeing time. So after three nights we politely said our goodbyes, jumped on the train and checked into a backpacker hostel in the heart of the city. Greenhouse Backpackers in Flinders Lane is on the sixth floor of a multi-storey office block and offers private accommodation as well as shared rooms and dormitories with shared bathrooms. It has a lift, a great rooftop terrace and laundry facilities. Best of all is the free continental breakfast and the once-a-week free pasta night!

Apart from the two nights we spent at the Civic in Townsville, we had no real experience of city hostel living and half-imagined some sort of seedy back-alley joint with leaky taps, dimly lit bathrooms, arrogant staff and shady, freeloading backpackers who were out of luck and out of money. Ambika was understandably a bit apprehensive and wondered aloud how I managed to talk her into these things in the first place. But one look at the Greenhouse facilities and all her fears were allayed. It was clean, well-organised and efficiently managed. With secure key card access, immaculately maintained rooms and spotless showers and toilets – it truly was the answer to the budget traveller's prayers. Our room was compact with a bunk bed, a small metal locker and a desk and chair. But no window. It looked a bit like an interrogation cell, but once the initial shock wore off, we didn't mind at all, especially as we planned to be out sightseeing every day.

We soon got into a routine and learnt quite a bit about hostel life. Each morning before we set off for the day, and with memories of 'milk thief Ilsa' still fresh in her mind, Ambika would scrutinise our fellow guests in the kitchen while I continued with my job search. She quickly discerned the two most important rules when it came to hostel living: if you don't tag your food, it's considered common property; and amenities are strictly 'first come, first served'. Of course, there were a variety of micro rules too – long-term residents got priority over short-term lodgers; condiments like oil, salt, sugar and, at a stretch, even butter and jam were considered 'transferable'; and pots, pans and cutlery were to be washed, dried and returned to their original place – without fail. But then there were grey areas which made things interesting: could dishcloths be used for cleaning cooktops? Could the butter knife be used in the jam jar? Who was responsible for topping up the sugar or coffee? Were slippers (or thongs, as the Aussies called them) allowed in the kitchen?

During our short stay at the Greenhouse, we witnessed some minor scuffles in the communal kitchen – but also casual flirtations and amorous advances! And of course we loved the free pasta night. The meal was half the fun though, the quirky habits of the hostelers provided ample entertainment – from eager mobs queuing up an hour before mealtime to guests trying to sneak back in for second helpings.

Our week in Melbourne flew by, and although we did a lot, a lack of time and money meant we couldn't do everything. We visited the spectacular Melbourne Museum, the largest in the southern hemisphere, located in the picturesque Carlton Gardens, also home to the imposing Royal Exhibition Building built in 1879. Strolling along the Gardens' tree-lined pathways flanked by sweeping lawns under the comforting shade of English oaks, poplars, elms, conifers and cedars was a rewarding experience in itself.

We also went on the City Parks Walk by the Yarra River, which takes you through four different parklands – the Alexandra Gardens, the Kings Domain, the Royal Botanic Gardens and the Queen Victoria Gardens. The immaculately maintained lawns and parklands are dotted with sculptures, statues, fountains, monuments and memorials. The path branches off in different directions revealing pockets of individually designed theme gardens, play areas and lakeside picnic spots. Most impressive, however, are the trees, shrubs and plants that create an oasis in the heart of a cosmopolitan city. Some of the giant trees that line the avenues were planted in the 1860s at the peak of the boom when the city got piped water for the first time.

We ended our long and leisurely walk that day at the Shrine of Remembrance in the Kings Domain on St Kilda Road just south of the town centre Opened in 1934, this grand memorial pays respect to the countless Australian men and women who lost their lives and serves as a sobering reminder of the cost of war. Just as we were climbing the Shrine's imposing front stairs, the mild temperatures and blue skies suddenly changed. Within seconds, dull grey clouds rolled in from the south and the rain came down. The glum weather seemed an appropriate backdrop for our visit to the shrine. The bronze statue of a soldier-father and son in the crypt represented the two generations of Australians who served in the two World Wars and invoked a particular sense of pain for the senseless loss of life. Originally built in honour of the men and women of Victoria who served in World War I, the memorial now functioned as a memorial to acknowledge all Australians who served in all the wars. We ventured out on the roof of the building, despite the whipping cold wind and the constant drizzle, to get a view of Melbourne city skyline which dominated the far side of the river.

We spent another afternoon exploring the city's historic shopping arcades and the downtown precinct, revelling in the potpourri of more than a hundred and forty cultures that co-exist harmoniously, giving the city its unique artistic, culinary, literary, musical and political flavour. Melbourne's eclectic dining scene is one of the best in the world and offers something to suit all tastes – fusion, traditional, exotic or homespun. If art is more your thing, you'll find it everywhere, from the countless public and private galleries, to the dizzying array of public sculpture and of course the buzzing laneways featuring walls covered in colourful graffiti and murals, and cool basement bars. Towards the end of our stay, we went on a romantic sunset date at the top of the Eureka Tower, the highest public vantage point in the southern hemisphere at 297 metres. Named after the Eureka Stockade gold rush rebellion in 1854, the Tower's observation deck offers spectacular views of the city and surrounds. It was a fitting end to our stay.

In just one week, Melbourne had captured our hearts and taken our breath away. It was indeed futile trying to resist her charming ways and wild mood swings, but we knew this would not be our final goodbye. Someday, we would return and relive our incredible experiences – next time with our children.

CHAPTER 19
Twelve Apostles

Adventure may hurt you, but monotony will kill you –
Unknown

Apart from being one of the most scenic drives in the world, Victoria's Great Ocean Road also happens to be the longest war memorial on the planet. What was once a mere rutted dirt track connecting far-flung pastoral outposts was painstakingly converted into a proper road in 1919 following thirteen years of hard work by a hardy contingent of World War I veterans. They dedicated the road to their comrades who were not so lucky and died on the battlefield.

The coastal route skirts the southernmost extremity of the Australian continent and includes a wide range of stunning natural scenery. With dramatic windswept views of the boisterous circumpolar Southern Ocean, the road twists and turns through rainforests, rolling hills, sheer limestone cliffs and secluded beaches. Mile for mile, this 300-kilometre stretch of road from the surf capital of Torquay to the historic fishing village of Port Fairy packs as much punch as an exotic thousand-mile fairyland expedition.

Indeed, in appearance, this part of Australia is not far removed from C.S. Lewis's mythical land of Narnia. While Narnia featured talking animals, the Great Ocean Road doesn't fall far behind in terms of the exotic.

The land is home to jacky lizards, short-beaked echidnas and swamp wallabies; the skies are ruled by sugar gliders, rufous fantails, superb fairywrens, yellow robins and grey shrike-thrushes; while the untamed seas abound with whales, little penguins and seals. It was easy to imagine Aslan, the King Lion, bounding from the forest cover!

Although we were fast running out of money, we decided to rent another car and drive this iconic coastal route at our leisure. Nearly 70 per cent of visitors from Melbourne opt for a day-trip on a charter bus, but we didn't consider this option. After exploring the Great Ocean Road and environs, we would then drive to Canberra, stopping overnight at the wineries in the Yarra Valley. From there we'd go to Sydney, which would mark the end of our road trip and our backpacking adventure. In a fortnight, if all went to plan, we would transition from being two carefree backpackers to homely migrants eager to find our place in Australian society.

Despite the GPS, it took us nearly an hour to find our way out of Melbourne and its daunting maze of interconnected highways and bypasses. This was an achievement in itself, and our enthusiasm levels surpassed that of school kids on an annual picnic. But as we approached the coastal town of Torquay, which marks the start of the Great Ocean Road, my enthusiasm got the better of me and I got a speeding fine. Unbeknown to me at that time, and mercifully so, I was five kilometres over the limit. The crushing $395 fine notice was delivered a month later. It was an atrociously large amount of money for a couple on a strict travel budget.

We decided to stay for two nights at Port Campbell, a colourful seaside village close to the Great Ocean Road's most famous landmark – the Twelve Apostles. The drive from Melbourne usually takes about three hours. However, along this coastal route, it's not about reaching your destination; the captivating landscapes beg to be explored. The real magic begins about 13 kilometres south when the Anglesea road ramps down past the coastal town of Torquay and the iconic Bells Beach, world-famous for its surf competitions and the birthplace of the iconic surfwear brands Rip

Twelve Apostles

Curl and Quiksilver. From here the two-lane road offers uninterrupted views of the rugged coastline and the densely wooded forests of the Otway National Park. Tall mountain ashes, giant beech, blackwood and eucalypts dot the coastline and the wet mountain gullies covered with fluorescent lichen and delicate ferns add a dreamlike quality.

We stopped at the quaint seaside town of Lorne, a prominent tourist spot with a Mediterranean-like setting that offers fresh sea air, white beaches and a vibrant community who take their lattes and their local art very seriously! Lunch was big juicy burgers on organic sourdough locally baked at the unapologetically assertive Bottle of Milk café – a local favourite not just for the lip-smacking food but also for the lively beach-town vibes and the eclectic crowd ranging from sun-soaked surf-chasers, affluent locals and intrepid travellers.

The road from Lorne hugs the coast until it makes a dramatic turn inland at Apollo Bay into the forested canopy of Cape Otway, before boomeranging a further 30 kilometres back to the coast at Glenaire. To the left lies the southern tip of this vast continent marked by the conspicuous white Cape Otway Lighthouse. Looking seaward we were rewarded with unimpeded views of the bight which marks the boundary of the infamous Shipwreck Coast.

We made a detour to the lighthouse, situated on a sprawling 200 acres of open grassy fields. I have always held these vital navigational aids in the highest regard, silent sentinels which have offered safe passage to countless ships since time immemorial. Their importance today, although diminished with the advent of modern radar technology and reliable nautical charts, can never be completely obliterated. For a sailor, seeing a beacon of light miles out to sea offers comfort during dark lonely nights. Lighthouses provide forlorn, homesick sailors with an emotional link with the land. I have spent many nights transiting unknown foreign coasts gazing nostalgically at the flashing beams of a lighthouse, having silent conversations with the lonely lighthouse keeper, and with the residents of the isolated seaside town near which it stands.

Cape Otway Lighthouse is the oldest surviving lighthouse in mainland Australia. Built in 1848, it sits atop towering sea cliffs with commanding views of Bass Strait and the Southern Ocean. Although decommissioned in 1994, its history tells a fascinating story of extreme hardships and incredible grit.

Charles La Trobe, the then superintendent of Port Phillip, chose the perfect vantage point from a ship master's perspective to build the lighthouse. But for the workers involved, the location proved to be challenging and inaccessible. Transporting sandstone by ox-carts through the impenetrable forests was no easy task. Nor were the logistical demands and the gruelling physical labour required in the harsh conditions. It took seventy men nearly ten months to construct the 21-metre structure. Yet, they built it to such exacting proportions that no cement was required. The transportation and installation of the twenty-one parabolic reflectors proved to be particularly challenging. Manufactured in London, the delicate pieces were ferried ashore in small boats through the crashing surf. When lit on 29 August 1848, the lighthouse became the beacon of hope for all ships that made the long and arduous voyage from England. For thousands of new arrivals, Cape Otway was their first sight of land after leaving Europe. For many captains, it was the saving grace when navigating these perilous coastlines. Originally the flame was lit by sperm whale oil until it was eventually replaced by electricity in 1939. The lighthouse marks a focal point of reference: 26,000 kilometres from England and 3600 kilometres from Antarctica.

With all our extra stops along the way, we ended up getting into Port Campbell towards sunset. We had pre-booked one of the cheapest rooms available at the Port Campbell Hostel which turned out to be a good move as the town was buzzing with visitors. A sleepy, pocket-sized seaside village, Port Campbell is the kind of place where it feels like time stands still. With a resident population of just six hundred, its mainstay is tourism and cray fishing. It's a kind of town where everyone is on a first-name basis, and locals look after each other; a community where probably the local doctor is also the local tour guide; the postman doubles as the handyman and pub talks revolve around the size of the daily catch and the mysterious disappearance of the mayor's cat. The community has one small petrol station which also doubles as the laundromat and fish and tackle store; a post office that shares the space with a souvenir shop; and a low-set red-brick Baptist church.

The Port Campbell Hostel is a modest single-storey brick structure located on Teagea Street less than 200 metres from the foreshore. It caters mainly to backpackers and budget travellers but also offers en suite family rooms. The communal kitchen and the dining area are large and bright. The hostel managers, a lovely old couple, showed us around and provided us with a set of house rules before handing us the keys to our room and a map of the town and surrounds. Our room was one of the smallest on offer with just enough space for a bunk bed, a small metal table and a portable electric heater. The toilet and shower facilities were shared, but Ambika was a hardened backpacker by this stage, and at just $50 per night, we weren't complaining.

The choice of restaurants and pubs in Port Campbell is limited, so we made our choice based on the number of patrons who were lining up for last-minute orders. We ended up going for pizza at Nico's, a traditional Italian pizzeria adorned with nostalgic paraphernalia from Italy – a Ferrari flag, postcards depicting rural Italian landscapes, vintage photos of Vespa scooters and Fiat cars, and flyers announcing traditional Italian shows or notable concerts.

After dinner we ambled along the foreshore and sat down on one of the park benches that overlook the bay. It was a quiet night with a cloudless sky alight with the brilliance of a million stars. You could almost taste the tanginess of the briny sea carried onshore by the chilly south-westerly. The sound of the waves was soothing. The large oily swells that rolled into the bay caught the reflection of the town lights. Yet, as most of the shipwrecked souls would testify, all this gave a false sense of safety to those who failed to realise the raw power of these cold and treacherous waters.

The jagged coastline with its vertical cliffs, hidden reefs, and off-lying islands made navigation a challenge; while the extreme weather conditions – dense fog, shrieking polar winds and stormy seas – made sailing an arduous and downright murderous affair. Ominously termed the Shipwreck

Coast, this part of Victoria contains around seven hundred shipwrecks scattered on the seabed.

Most shipwrecks occurred in the mid- to late 1800s when the wooden vessels transporting ill-fated convicts and hopeful settlers alike were arriving in large numbers. This was well before the advent of steamships and lighthouses. It was a time when bold captains and diehard sailors pitted their wits against the vagaries of the seas. Most of the ships were able to conclude their voyage with minor incidents; however, some were not so lucky, meeting an untimely and unceremonious end. The cruellest part of such disasters was many succumbed just a few miles from the coastline, often within sight of land, after their perilous 10,000-mile journey.

If you listen closely enough, you can hear the tormented cries of the hundreds of mariners seeking help and respite from the icy cold and the crushing depths. 'I have seldom seen a more fearful section of coastline,' wrote Matthew Flinders, the explorer who first mapped the coast of Australia. Standing at the edge of this vast continent, I gazed deep into the bosom of the sea and offered prayers to my fellow sailors and to all those who met with a tragic end. I also offered my gratitude to the sea gods for keeping me safe throughout my career. Life at sea had made me a stronger and more resourceful person; it had also made me more acceptable and accommodating to my fellow seafarers and the world at large. I was privileged to have been offered rare glimpses of the ocean's veiled tenderness and captivating beauty and to have witnessed some wondrous and magical natural sights – a sailor's greatest reward for the sacrifices of being away from family and society. The timid young cadet who boarded a ship decades ago had returned ashore as a changed man more at peace and in tune with his inner self.

Early the next day, we set off for the experience of a lifetime and one of the highlights of our trip – a privately chartered helicopter ride over the majestic Twelve Apostles. Located about 10 kilometres away from Port Campbell, the 12 Apostles Helicopters hangar sits opposite the expansive and interactive visitor centre. Costing around $300, we had to dig deep in our wallets to retrieve the dog-eared hundred-dollar bills purposefully set aside as a contingency fund. We were nearing the end of our journey and decided to splurge on this experience. We were not disappointed!

After a brief safety induction, Stan, our pilot, escorted us to the sleek H135 Airbus twin-seater helicopter and strapped us in. It was a crisp and crystal-clear day with not a cloud in sight. After safety checks, there was a further set of instructions from Stan, and then with a flick of the tail and a silent whirr of rotor blades, we were airborne. The aircraft nosed upwards as it rose to the flying altitude of 500 feet before banking and gliding away from the mainland in a south-easterly direction. We were instantly rewarded with breathtaking views of the verdant rural countryside. Vast farmlands, lush green pastures, sprawling acreages and rolling hills stretched as far as the eye could see. The black-asphalted Great Ocean Road almost appeared out of place in the stunning landscape.

Once over the sea, the helicopter steadied on a westerly course running parallel to the coastline and gave us a great view of the formidable Shipwreck Coast and the outlying Apostles. Below us, the long ocean swells rhythmically rolled into shore, piling up on top of each other as they met with resistance for the first time on their journey from the frozen depths of the Antarctic Sea. The pilot highlighted the various rock formations as we passed them: the Twelve Apostles, the Loch Ard Gorge, London Bridge, the Sentinel, the Grotto, Two Mile Bay and Point Hesse.

The Twelve Apostles were never really twelve to begin with; in fact, they were not even known as the Twelve Apostles when first sighted by the British. The early explorers called the limestone formations the 'Sow and Piglets'; the Sow was Mutton Bird Island, which stands at the mouth of Loch Ard Gorge, while her Piglets were the tall limestone stacks. In a calculated move, the local tourism board renamed the stacks in the 1920s to give them a more international appeal.

At last count, there were seven in the offshore cluster. They formed following natural erosion: a testimony of the might and relentless pounding of the monster waves of the Southern Ocean and the raging winds that prevail in these latitudes. These natural forces carved the soft limestone to form caves in the cliffs, which then became arches, which in turn collapsed; leaving towering stacks some 70 metres above sea level. Waves along this stretch of coast can reach up to 20 metres in height, and it's no wonder that so many of the old sailing ships failed to execute the last leg of the voyage.

One of the most poignant shipwreck stories was that of the clipper *Loch Ard* in June 1878. The clipper had departed England under the command of Captain Gibb in March of that year. Onboard were seventeen crew, thirty-seven passengers and a cargo of assorted goods. On 1 June, the ship was approaching Melbourne and expecting to sight land when it encountered dense fog. Unable to see the Cape Otway Lighthouse or gauge his distance off the coast, Gibb grossly miscalculated his position and drifted way off course.

At 4 a.m. on that day, the fog lifted to reveal, to Gibb's horror, that the vessel was just metres away from the off-lying breakers and the cliff face of the mainland. Within a matter of minutes, the ship ran aground on the reef, the impact of the waves smashing the fragile hull into smithereens. Of the fifty-four hapless souls on board, just two survived: Tom Pearce, an apprentice sailor, and Eva Carmichael. Tom managed to swim ashore, but he heard Eva's cries as she clung desperately to floating wreckage. He valiantly dived back into the murderous sea and pulled her to safety. The place where they finally stepped ashore is now known as Loch Ard Gorge. The perilous sea voyages may have been one of the reasons free settlers decided to stay back in Australia despite the hardship and uncertainty faced by the colonies in those early days.

Our helicopter ride lasted for about half an hour and was indeed a highlight of our trip. Later that day, we checked out the visitor centre which is run by a host of enthusiastic guides. We then took a walk along the beautifully maintained boardwalk to the Gibson Steps which lead down to the beach. On the shore, after dipping our toes in the freezing southern waters, we could fully appreciate the size and magnificence of the Apostles. Behind us was the sheer cliff face of the mainland, the gold-honey tones of the rock face glowing in the afternoon sun. It was a glorious – but treacherous – part of the world.

CHAPTER 20

The Valley of Fine Wines

I always wonder why birds stay in the same place when they can fly anywhere on earth. Then I ask myself the same question — Harun Yahya

Not a soul stirred as we awoke in the pre-dawn darkness to prepare for our departure from Port Campbell. Our next destination was Healesville, a suburb in the Yarra Valley north-east of Melbourne — a trip of about 350 kilometres. We gathered our bags and tiptoed to the reception area to drop off our keys then scurried into the kitchen like two timid mice to grab our breakfast of cereal and cold milk. While packing away the remainder of the food in our bag, we noticed a label marked 'Free to Share' on one of the fridge shelves. The shelf held a few leftovers from earlier hostel guests, and so we took a half-opened packet of raisin toast which would tide us over on our road trip. Taking the bread did not come naturally though, and we half-expected the sirens to go off, to our mortal embarrassment. Nothing happened, of course, and at that moment we felt as if we had earned another backpacker badge of honour.

We decided to drive back along the Great Ocean Road although there was a shorter alternate inland route. With Ambika at the wheel, we left Port Campbell just as the sun rose over the horizon, bathing the landscape in golden hues. Wisps of morning mist wafted onto the road from the adjacent farms, forming eddies in the crosswinds. A mob of wallabies bounded along just ahead of us, and Ambika stopped the car to let them pass. One little joey paused in the middle of the road casting a curious stare at us, oblivious to the danger. It was a fitting goodbye to this beautiful region. Unable to resist the urge, we stopped numerous times at several locations – besides green meadows and windswept beaches – enjoying the uplifting sights and the freshness of the fading winter chill.

We passed the northern edge of Melbourne and arrived at Research around midday. The historic town that initially served as an outpost for prospectors and miners in the 1800s was now the centre of the hugely popular Yarra Valley 'enotourism' region. Located in the beautiful valley of the Watts River, the town is surrounded on several sides by the stunning mountains of the Great Dividing Range, Australia's most substantial mountain range. Stretching more than 3500 kilometres from the north-eastern tip of Queensland, these ranges run along the entire length of the eastern coastline through New South Wales and Victoria before finally fading into the central plain at the Grampians. This unique feature of a sharp rise between the coastal lowlands and the eastern uplands has a big influence on the climate in the region. The First Fleet may have been lucky to unintentionally choose the most suitable area for settlement, but it was no fluke that 85 per cent of Australians continued to live under the canopy of the mighty ranges on the eastern coastline. The milder climate and increased water resources were in sharp contrast to the dry, arid landscape of much of the rest of Australia.

Our stopover in Research was as much about necessity as anything else. Canberra is roughly 900 kilometres from Melbourne, and we thought it prudent to break up our journey. A sleepover at the doorstep of one of Australia's most beautiful wine regions seemed the most appealing choice. We were only staying a night and we were lucky to find an accommodation close to the winery triangle bound by the towns of Coldstream, Healesville and Yarra Glen.

Nadia and Rafael, our Airbnb hosts, were out in the backyard when we arrived. They welcomed us warmly and we exchanged a few pleasantries as we entered their house. Nadia's parents had migrated to Australia from Europe in the late 1960s in search of a better life and never went back. Rafael's parents, on the other hand, had migrated from Chile intending to live in Australia for just a few years and to improve their language skills. In the meantime, Rafael was born and political unrest in Chile resulted in them deciding to stay permanently. Both Nadia and Rafael grew up in capital cities and had moved to Research because of their businesses. They were curious to learn about our story of life back in India, our migration and our current road trip. We asked Nadia how she felt about living in Australia.

'Rafael and I have travelled to many countries over the years, both independently and together. While we would consider living somewhere else temporarily, it's highly unlikely we would consider migrating anywhere permanently. We love living here and all our family is here. Besides, we had the most carefree and happy upbringing as kids, and I truly believe that this country is second to none for that.' As if on cue, the main door of the house opened, and their three children, Dante, Alejandro, and Josette, came bounding out, trying to outrace each other to the backyard.

Nadia showed us our room which was on the lower level of the large cream-coloured Queenslander-style house. It was spacious with a bathroom, a large double bed, a bar fridge and a side table with an electric kettle. It opened onto the lovely backyard. A foosball table straddled the centre of the room, and a wooden library filled up a corner space – the shelves stacked with books of all sizes and genres. As we were only staying one night, we unpacked just the bare essentials, jumped into the car and embarked upon our quest for some premium chardonnay.

We drove around the valley for about an hour enjoying the landscape and wound up at the sprawling Chateau Yering vineyard – one of the first wineries of this region. With the first vines planted in 1838, the Yarra

Valley became Victoria's first wine-growing district. Back then the Scottish-born Ryrie brothers, moving their cattle south from Sydney, took up a grazing licence of 43,000 acres and adopted the name 'Yering', the Aboriginal name for the area. They planted two grape varietals but mainly used the land for grazing their cattle. In 1845 the first Yarra Valley wine was made by James Dardel. During the early 1850s, Paul de Castella took over Yering and transformed the cattle station into a landmark of winemaking in Victoria. Yering Station was purchased by the Rathbone family in 1996 and it continues to be a family-owned and operated winery. The entrance to the vineyard is lined with tall eucalypts and gum trees while the estate grounds feature the distinctive rows of vines drooping under the weight of mature grapes. The feel of exclusivity, tradition and brass-polished grandeur is hard to miss – from the original 1859 brick structure to the stern lines of the modern stone and glass building that houses the fine-dining restaurant with expansive views of the Yarra Ranges. For wealthy tourists, the estate offers exclusive flights aboard a privately owned Superlite helicopter.

Sadly, we are not wine connoisseurs and did not have the cash to splurge on the $100 three-course sit-down meal in the restaurant – let alone another helicopter ride! We instead followed the day-trippers into the century-old brick building which houses the estate's cellar and wine store. The tasting room is just past the wine store in a large rectangular room with high cathedral ceilings, devoid of any furniture save a few tables made from oak barrels. In the centre of the tasting room, with easy access to all four corners, is the main bar. The charming hostesses were tirelessly filling the wine glasses with Yering's signature chardonnays, pinots, rosés and sparkling wines. Most of the visitors were making the most of the session and so Ambika and I joined in. Ambika got into the thick of it, trying to understand the finer details. The hostess was throwing around words like 'colour', 'nose' and 'palate' as well as terms like 'green tints', 'nashi pear' and 'vanillin oak spice'. I was onto my fourth wine by then, grinning sheepishly, and couldn't make head nor tail of it. We left after an hour or so as we needed to return to Research and get an early night. We were leaving for Canberra at 5 a.m. the next morning.

Back at our Airbnb house, our hosts were in the backyard hosting a dinner party for some family friends. Rafael had fired up the barbecue while the kids were having a field day running around, mimicking swordplay, jumping on the trampoline, and doing a great job of ignoring the grown-ups. This was Australian living as I had imagined it. A sprawling house with whitewashed exteriors, manicured lawns with boisterous kids playing in the garden, the lip-smacking aromas of a home-cooked barbecue meal wafting on the cool evening breeze – a life of contentment, security and abundance. We hadn't seen much of Australia yet – or maybe we'd been lucky – but everything thus far filled our hearts with gladness and hope.

Nadia and Rafael kindly invited us to join them for dinner, but we didn't want to impose. Besides, we had a very early start the next morning. Just as we were saying our goodnights and goodbyes, Nadia asked if we knew about the daylight-saving time due to take effect at the stroke of midnight. We didn't and it now meant that we would be waking up at the ungodly hour of 3 a.m.!

CHAPTER 21

Seat of Power

Travel is more than the seeing of sights; it is a change that goes on, deep and permanent, in the ideas of living – Miriam Beard

We drove at a leisurely pace along the modern Hume Highway – which links Melbourne with Sydney - and covered the 600-kilometre road trip in eight hours, reaching Giralang, an outer suburb of Canberra, around noon. Our Airbnb host Amanda's house was a two-storey brick bungalow that sat high on an elevated block of land with commanding views of the neighbourhood. The top floor was Amanda's primary residence, but she rented out a couple of modified self-contained rooms in the lower section. She showed us our room which opened onto a traditional fenced backyard. We unpacked, got cleaned up and immediately headed out to explore the sights of Australia's capital city.

When Australia's separate colonies federated to form the Commonwealth in 1901, the intense competition and rivalry between Sydney and Melbourne posed a unique challenge – which city should be crowned the nation's capital? There was no clear winner so after much deliberation, a decision was made that neither would be chosen as the seat of power and all eyes turned to a dusty, rural stretch of land which lay halfway between the two cities. In 1913, the site where Canberra now sits was little more than a sprawling sheep station. The first surveyor of the area had a specific set of instructions – to find an attractive setting for 'a beautiful city ... embracing distinctive features ... worthy of the object, not only for the present but for all time.'

The newly formed Australian nation was riding high on a wave of success and was eager to dazzle the world. The founding fathers (and mothers!) had a grand vision for the capital city and, in a strategic move, conducted an international design competition to create a blueprint for the 'official and social centre of Australia'. Canberra would be the first properly planned city in the country.

The government delegated the naming of the new capital to the Australian citizens. Over seven hundred suggestions were received. Although 'Canberra' was the clear frontrunner – the name derives from a local Aboriginal word for 'meeting place' – there were plenty of creative alternatives like 'Cookaburra', 'Wheatwoolgold' and 'Kangaremu'. Then there were ridiculous suggestions like 'Sydmelperadbrisho' and 'Meladneyperbane', and the politically motivated 'Swindleville', 'Gonebroke' and 'Caucus City'. If nothing else, the exercise proved that the young nation had an imagination and a sense of humour! Fortunately, the powers-that-be decided to take the more conservative route, and the site was officially christened Canberra on 12 March 1913 by Lady Denham, the wife of Governor-General.

The city's design competition garnered significant interest worldwide and in 1912, American architect Walter Burley Griffin's plan was chosen. Griffin's winning design showed an artistic grasp of town planning with a chain of lakes along the Molonglo Valley and a triangular city framework encompassed by the surrounding mountain ranges. It was a simple yet splendid concept, laid out in an attractive geometric pattern based on circles and rectangles joined by long tree-lined avenues and boulevards which enhanced the valley's natural landscape. It was claimed that Griffin's design would create 'the only modern city in the world'. Although construction started in 1918, by late 1920, Griffin had left – a victim of unbending administration and his own uncompromising, creative genius – when barely any construction work had been completed. The effects of war and recession added to the delays and the legislature did not move until 1927. Australia officially recognised Griffin's work in 1964 when Canberra's central lake was filled, just as Griffin had intended. The then Prime Minister Robert Menzie named it Lake Burley Griffin, making it the first 'monument' in Canberra dedicated to the city's designer.

The creation of Canberra was not without critics – some cynics said it was a 'waste of a good sheep pasture'. According to another, the city 'is an example of how planning, on the rare occasions when it is done thoroughly, mostly results in something we scorn'. And, 'Canberra is a place with no sense of community, with an automotive footprint and hardly any people. [It] has no urbanistic qualities: it's an antisocial city in denial of people with feet.' Ouch!

To be honest, our initial reaction mirrored the critics'! Our first drive around town was on the afternoon of our arrival. It was a Sunday and I didn't expect much activity in a place mostly inhabited by bureaucrats, politicians and government servants getting ready for the week ahead. What surprised me was the lack of *any* activity. In the half-hour drive into the city centre, we saw no pedestrians, nor anything you'd expect to see – street-side cafés, restaurants, souvenir shops, country pubs. No one was strolling along the roads, there were no corner shops, and no kids riding bikes on the footpaths. The streets, the overlapping freeways and the tall government buildings that we passed appeared insipid, functional and lacking any vibe.

Only when we reached the northern shores of Lake Burley Griffin and the bordering Commonwealth Park did we see any real signs of activity. Families, large and small, were spread around, enjoying late afternoon picnics. The evening breeze carried the floral fragrance from the Floriade exhibition, Canberra's annual flower and entertainment festival that celebrates the Australian spring. A large water-jet in the centre of the lake discharged a tall stream over 100 metres into the sky; the water spray carried away in whichever direction the wind blew. Installed to commemorate the bicentenary of Captain Cook's landing, the jet was grand but missed the mark in terms of aesthetics. It seemed nothing more than a water cannon with immense grunt no doubt, but with no real purpose. A tall water fountain cascading over white marble sculptures or bronze figurines would have achieved so much more, I thought to myself.

On the opposite shore, the sun's rays cast long shadows on the national monuments – the old Parliament House, the National Portrait Gallery, the National Library and scores of other imposing structures which unfortunately were too distant to cast any real impression from the 'civilian' side of the river. The reality of Canberra was that it looked great on paper – the circular avenues, expansive gardens and vast open spaces carved into geometric shapes by broad leafy thoroughfares had a pleasing symmetry – however, at ground level, the architectural splendour was lost on visitors, and the Parliamentary zone seemed to be an endless labyrinth of empty streets that discouraged pedestrian activity. As it was a late Sunday afternoon, we didn't expect to have much luck visiting any memorials or galleries, so we took the opportunity to drive around the quiet State Circular Drive and surrounds and took in the sights of the numerous monuments, international embassies and the War Memorial.

The highlight of our visit was the guided tour of Parliament House, the heart of Australian democracy, which we did the next day. Lying at the epicentre of the city, the impressive boomerang-shaped building was opened in 1988 by Queen Elizabeth II. With the towering 81-metre flagpole dominating the skyline, the building was not constructed to express power as most such structures around the world inadvertently do. In true Australian spirit, it was built *into* a hill, not on top of it, to symbolise that the government is never above the people.

The design brief was unimaginable; so large in fact that the exhaustive list of criteria spanned twenty volumes and formed a pile about a metre high. The architects had to adhere to stringent requirements with a strong emphasis on including elements of the unique Australian landscape. Ninety per cent of the materials used in the construction were sourced from within Australia.

We joined a late afternoon tour, not knowing what to expect, and were impressed before we even walked across the expansive forecourt, which is covered with a mesmerising dot-patterned Aboriginal mosaic depicting the Western Desert Dreaming. The sheer bush granite columns of the Great Verandah towered over us as we approached the entrance. Overhead, the massive Australian flag fluttered majestically in the gentle spring breeze, and the tall stainless steel pole pierced the blue skies.

Phil, our tour guide for the afternoon, was gathering the visitors together in the building's magnificent marble foyer. There was a buzz of activity all around; tour groups huddled together shepherded by expert guides; administrative staff going about their daily business; stern-looking security guards patrolling the vast interiors. It was easy to forget that we were in fact in a functional parliament building with 4500 rooms and an equal number of staff who worked in the cavernous interiors on a sitting day. Somewhere in the labyrinth of this political powerhouse, decisions were made that shaped the nation's future.

The forty-minute tour, although rushed, was informative and entertaining. As it was a non-sitting day, we were allowed to view both chambers. Phil's insider stories and insights put things in context. The red colour scheme of the Senate chamber, for example, matches the House of Lords in London. However, the colours were modified to tints of ochre, suggestive of the Australian outback. Seventy-six senators sit in the Upper House, which is partly modelled on the US system, and has an equal representation of twelve people from each state and two each from the Northern Territory and the Australian Capital Territory.

'Do you know why the coat of arms has a kangaroo and an emu holding the shield that depicts the six state symbols?' Phil asked the group.

'Because they're Australian animals?' a German lady asked in a thick accent.

'Well, that's true,' Phil replied, 'but there's more to it.'

A young Australian boy raised his hand eagerly. 'Because they're some of the largest animals in Australia and the only ones that can lift such a heavy shield!'

'Well, that's true as well!' Phil said. 'But the main reason these animals have been tasked with such an important role is that neither of them can walk backwards ... and that, my dear friends, is a symbolic representation of our forwarding moving nation. As a side note,' he added, lowering his voice conspiratorially, 'it's claimed that the kangaroo holding the shield always has to be a male.'

As we were ushered into the House of Representatives or the Lower House, Phil explained a little bit about the political structure in Australia and the role of the Governor-General. The seemingly mid-level title is in fact the Queen's representative in Australia and holds a position of great power. Apart from being Australia's Head of State with a range of constitutional and ceremonial duties, the Governor-General is also the Commander-in-Chief of the Australian Defence Force. In layman's terms, he's the third umpire who gets called in to adjudicate on all the borderline decisions or in case of a political deadlock!

The colour scheme of the Lower House reflects the green associated with the British Parliament's House of Commons, but it also reflects the eucalypt green of the Australian bush. In both houses, the colours are the deepest at ground level and become lighter as they extend upwards. Many significant turning points in Australian history have been announced and debated in this room, and we felt privileged to be offered a glimpse.

Phil told us of an unusual problem that presented itself in the early days of the Australian Parliament. Traditionally, bells ring throughout the building for a few minutes before a scheduled session of Parliament to call members to the chambers. Green lights flash to indicate the call is for members of the House of Representatives; red lights are used to call senators. The question of what constituted a 'reasonable time' in the new building was posed.

'There was a big debate about this,' Phil explained. 'Many argued that the new Parliament House was just too big and members would take a long time to make it to the houses, depending on where they were. So they came up with an unconventional but effective plan: a senior politician was chosen and sent to the furthest corner of the building. The members then rang the bells and set the timer. The politician took a little under five minutes to reach the House, and the consensus for five minutes as a reasonable time was decided upon.'

After showing us around the Parliament's impressive art collection, Phil then led us to the Great Hall, a venue for formal receptions, state dinners and significant national events. The stunning Great Hall Tapestry designed by the famous Australian artist Arthur Boyd dominates the Hall. Woven in four separate pieces, the tapestry is the largest of its kind in the country and measures twenty metres wide by nine metres high. Rather than depicting a heroic scene or majestic panorama, the design evokes the textures and colours of the eucalypt forest – the continent's primary landscape.

After the tour, we spent some time in the majestic foregrounds digesting the wealth of information we'd just heard. I was amazed at how easy it was to gain access to one of the most vital institutions in this nation; during sitting days you are allowed to watch Question Time, see bills being debated, and sit in on committee inquiries as current issues are explored in detail.

As I looked north across the manicured gardens and past the Old Parliament House over to the other side of the lake, a realisation hit me – Canberra is not meant to be compared with any other city in Australia, and there is no flaw in its design or purpose. Its sights are enshrined within its magnificent institutions. To look for them outside is futile. The city safeguards the nation's history and preserves its wealth within the numerous world-class institutions, museums, galleries and archives, and it does so openly and transparently. The riches of the nation, its proud heritage, its many mistakes, its stellar achievements and its many challenges are laid bare – to be scrutinised, challenged, appreciated by all, and to help inform the next wave of decision-makers. Ambika and I looked forward to coming back to this lovely city along with our children one day in the future to delve further into Australia's rich history.

But our time was almost up. Our penultimate destination was the Blue Mountains on the outer fringes of Sydney's urban sprawl. Although we could have taken the quickest and most direct route via the M31, we opted for the more circuitous and winding Taralga Highway which would take us via Oberon and the central tablelands and, if we timed it right, the millennia-old Jenolan Caves.

CHAPTER 22

Dark Caves and New Discoveries

Adventure is a path ... your body will collide with the earth, and you will bear witness ... Nothing will ever again be black and white – Mark Jenkins

My alarm went off at 3.45 a.m. with a muted electronic beep. Ambika stirred dreamily and drew the blanket over her head as I crept from the bed and tiptoed into the lounge room. Outside, the wind was howling like a tormented animal, and the drooping leaves of the misshapen gum trees swayed noisily. Not a single star was visible in the night sky; all I could see was the edges of towering rain clouds, glowing like dying embers in the watery moonlight. A cold front had passed through overnight, and the day promised to be wet and miserable.

The steady rain had turned the pavement outside slick and translucent under the glare of the streetlights. Getting our bags into the car in the biting cold wind was a challenge, and I was soaked by the time I'd gone back and forth from the house three times. This did not dampen my spirits, but I could hear my teeth chattering.

Dawn broke as we left Amanda's; by this stage the rain had developed a predictable rhythm. The weather seemed to set the mood for our drive: the overcast skies and rain formed a perfect backdrop as we drove past villages and towns that bore an uncanny resemblance to the English countryside.

The distance to Katoomba, the main town in the Blue Mountains and our next stop, was around 330 kilometres; however, the route we chose would keep us to the west of the Great Dividing Range and the tablelands, and the narrow roads had many winding sections which would make the drive challenging, especially on a rainy day. The final part of the drive closer to Jenolan Caves would be especially demanding with its steep inclines and hairpin bends. We had planned a sightseeing stopover there but had to be judicious about the time if we were to make it to Katoomba by sunset. Driving anywhere in outback Australia in the dark is dangerous – not just because you might hit a wombat, an emu, kangaroo or a cow, but also because you might be waiting a very long time for help if something were to happen. I decided to take it carefully.

The Taralga Road begins at Goulburn at the M31 junction, linking Oberon with Bathurst, a historical town that was the first inland settlement in Australia. It was also the place where gold was first discovered. The backroad passes through dreamy, picturesque landscapes; verdant pastures, quiet hamlets, and rolling hills covered with a carpet of bright green grass.

The area in the vicinity of the Abercrombie National Park, especially where the river passes under the wooden bridge near the Bummaroo Ford campgrounds, is particularly mesmerising. Here open forests of inland scribbly gum, eucalypts and stringy red barks compete for space, while along the riverbed, the tall river oaks, tea trees and bottlebrushes provide an ideal ground cover for the native wildlife. The crisp country air carried the earthy fragrance of the pastures – the whiff of rain mingled with the distinct scents of unspoilt foliage.

We drove along the deserted roads, our music blaring and our windows rolled down. On one occasion, I stopped at the side of the road to relieve myself beside a large paddock that was hemmed in by low wooden posts. We were listening to our favourite collection of Hindi tracks and humming away to 'Ale', a catchy song from the Bollywood movie *Golmaal*, when a curious thing happened. As I stood by the fence attending to my business, a herd of cows who were grazing peacefully nearby came over. It seemed a bright blue car, two lonesome travellers and thumping music merited a closer inspection on an otherwise ordinary day. Maybe it was just our minds playing tricks on us, but I swear we saw the herd distinctly swaying to the beats of the song in unison, their bells and swishy tails flapping in opposite directions. We were so excited to have an audience and to have had such an effect on these bovine creatures that we cranked up the volume and decided to show them our dance moves. We must have struck quite a sight – us gyrating on the roadside, and the cows swaying on the other side of the fence. Of course, they may have just have been hungry and mistook us for farmers! But I prefer to think they were enjoying the music.

The well-tended paddocks, the fertile grazing pastures and the numerous farms we saw that day are testimony to the early pioneers who risked their lives to venture so far inland from Sydney. Those early explorers had to find suitable land for the expanding colonies, and it was only due to the sheer determination and persistence that they broke through their 'ecological isolation' and crossed the seemingly impassable mountain range to the west of Sydney.

The Blue Mountains had been hoodwinking settlers from the time of Captain Cook's landing in 1770 right through to 1813. Due to the rough terrain, they were seen as a barrier to future exploration and expansion. The range gets its name because of the distinctive blue haze – a result of finely dispersed droplets of oil from the eucalypts combining with dust particles and water vapour, resulting in short-wave rays of 'blue' light. Between 1789 and 1806, ten expeditions attempted to breach this natural fortress; most of these forays were deemed heroic failures.

At the same time, on the other side of the world, the Industrial Revolution had taken Europe by storm in the 1760s and had given that part of the world a whole new direction. Most European countries were transitioning from being predominantly agriculture-based societies to ones driven by industry. This revolution was led by Great Britain – Australia's faraway kingdom – and marked a significant turning point in the history of human society. In Australia, however, the very existence of the colony hung in the balance. If suitable land wasn't found quickly, the population might have perished. The colonists had nothing more than pickaxes and shovels to work with, unlike their counterparts across Europe who were far advanced in comparison.

The Blue Mountains stopped everyone in their tracks, and the task seemed hopeless. In the early 1800s, the British House of Commons glibly concluded that beyond these indomitable mountains, 'the colony will not be capable of extension'.

But then in 1813 three hardy explorers made a concerted effort to release Sydney from its topographical prison. The three men were Gregory Blaxland, William Lawson and William Wentworth. Along with four servants, four pack horses and five dogs, they set off on an exploration which was to create history. On 11 May 1813, they left Emu Plains and reached the foothills of the Blue Mountains, or Glenbrook, as it is known today. The trip was tough. The party had insufficient food, and the trek required constant hacking through thick scrub and navigating 'damp dew-laden undergrowth'. Fear of attack by Aborigines was ever-present, but the men soldiered on regardless. Eighteen days later, on 29 May 1813, they discovered the gently sloping mountains to the west of the ranges and on 31 May 1813, after weeks of a laborious excursion across 93 kilometres of harsh terrain, they finally managed to break through the pass. They climbed a sugar-loaf shaped hill and saw the most beautiful sight – vast plains and fertile lands that stretched as far as the eye could see. Blaxland exclaimed, 'Forest or grassland, sufficient in extent … to support the stock of the colony for the next thirty years.' Today, just west of Katoomba, you can see the remains of a eucalyptus tree marked by the famous explorers Blaxland, Wentworth and Lawson, one of the only remnants of this landmark event.

This was a watershed moment in Australia's colonial history, and the farmers and pastoralists were quick to pack up and move to these farmlands, venturing even further afield as time progressed.

The last 20 kilometres from Oberon to the Jenolan Caves proved to be the most hair-raising. Edith Road passes high country farmland before descending dramatically via a series of hairpin bends. The surrounding forests of snow gum and mountain gum hem the narrow road in a tight embrace. In a short distance, we rose nearly 430 metres as we first climbed up the western edges of the mountain range and then descended equally rapidly about 700 metres to the valley floor.

The Jenolan Caves are the oldest limestone caves in the world and it's thought they formed around 340 million years ago. They were discovered by white settlers in 1838 when the local authorities stumbled upon the hidden valley by chance while chasing a convict! One can only imagine how many more ancient secrets lay hidden across this vast continent. With just over two hundred years of colonisation, and a meagre population spread thinly across an enormous undiscovered continent, it was unsurprising for people to discover, stumble upon, walk into, dig up or chance upon new finds all the time.

The Caves network follows the course of a subterranean section of the Jenolan River, and features more than 40 kilometres of multi-level passages and over three hundred entrances. The region is so massive and widely spread out that exploration is still being done even today. Tourists can take guided tours through caves with imaginative names like Temple of Baal, Imperial Diamond, and Pool of Cerberus. After the initial discovery in 1838, more caves kept being found over the next sixty-five years. This is probably the only place in the world with an appointed 'Keeper of the Cave' tasked with preserving the integrity and beauty of the network. The caves were opened to tourists early on, but there was little control over visitors who damaged these ancient rock formations, pilfering souvenirs and writing graffiti on the bedrock. Mercifully, such profanity was brought to a stop in 1872 and in 1884 the name 'Jenolan Caves' was adopted.

Every cave has something to offer, and tours depart at regular intervals throughout the day. Some excursions are easily accessible while others are extremely demanding and require a certain measure of dexterity and physical fitness. For the adventurous, there are numerous adventure caving

Dark Caves and New Discoveries

activities where participants don overalls, helmets and headlamps before venturing into the dark depths.

The Chifley Cave tour, for example, is rated for people with an average fitness level and is relatively easy to navigate. It features some of the most striking limestone formations, including the exquisite 'spar' crystal. This was the first cave and one of the earliest places in the world to be lit with electric light back in 1880 – a remarkable achievement at the time.

We arrived around mid-morning and with little time to spare, joined a tour of the Temple of Baal cave. We were tingling with excitement. Our group of twelve huddled at the entrance while our tour guide Jack, a stocky man in a khaki uniform, greeted us and provided us with the customary safety briefing and a short introduction. As we descended via a long tunnel, Jack deftly switched on the passage lights with a pocket remote, and we were instantly transported back in time to the age of the early explorers. Jack was an entertaining guide and timed his pauses and content delivery masterfully. The evocative sound and light effects were used to maximum effect to highlight the features of the cave, and there was a gasp of amazement every time this occurred. The crystalline formations sparkled like distant stars in the glow of the lights, and the enormous stalactites and stalagmites added an other-worldly feel to the experience.

As we descended the 'Dragon's Throat' via a winding staircase, we entered two enormous chambers, one of which is 42 metres tall, filled with some of the most beautiful limestone formations we'd ever seen. One of these formations, the 9-metre-tall 'Angel's Wing' shawl, is one of the largest ever discovered in the world. There were many more of such formations, their names keeping to the biblical theme: Red Altar, Jason and Ram, to name a few.

We completed our ninety-minute tour around noon and after a quick lunch made haste for Katoomba about 70 kilometres away. We were looking forward to seeing the famous Blue Mountains before our final destination, Sydney.

CHAPTER 23

Into the Blue

Our happiest moments as tourists always seem to come when we stumble upon one thing while in pursuit of something else – Lawrence Block

Lou's house was a rustic two-storey cedar house painted in earth-brown colours and topped with a green corrugated iron roof. Planter boxes suspended below the front window ledges contained petunias, as yet unflowering. By the front door, a row of Tibetan prayer flags that adorned the porch fluttered in the afternoon breeze.

Inside, the spacious floorplan opened up into the main lounge area and then a modern kitchen. The house had minimal furniture – a couch and lazy boy fronting a small flat-screen TV sitting on a yellow display unit, a four-seater lounge and a log fireplace. One wall in the living room had been converted into a rock-climbing practice wall. Two bookshelves were bursting at the seams. The house's best feature was the French doors which opened up onto a large elevated back deck, allowing the sunlight to stream inside. The views were breathtaking – tall pines, dense eucalypts, sloping gullies and the vast Blue Mountains National Park beyond.

Upstairs, the cosy guest bedroom had a double bed, a side table, a footstool and a bookshelf. A handwoven tapestry depicting the Indian Elephant God Ganesha hung on one wall – a giveaway that our hosts Lou or Steve either had been to India before or had some Indian connection.

So far we'd stayed with ten Airbnb hosts in Australia and had ten incredible experiences. The people we'd met and the experiences we shared had made our trip. The homestays had provided us with a local flavour and in almost all cases, turned strangers into friends. Our Katoomba hosts were no different.

Lou and Steve were not your typical Monday-to-Friday, nine-to-five working couple. Sick of the corporate rat race and the pressures of big city living, they gave up their home in Sydney and moved to the Blue Mountains. Lou worked at the Botanical Gardens as a visitor experience manager, while Steve was a volunteer fireman who also managed his home brewery. Lou loved rock climbing, hiking and adventure activities while Steve looked a bit like an army private. His most striking attribute, however, was his disarming smile and mild mannerisms which put us instantly at ease.

'The cost of living, the travel time and the daily pressures in Sydney were just too much,' Lou said. 'We were burning out quickly and knew that the lifestyle would not be sustainable. Housing affordability was another concern. For the price of a small one-bedroom unit close to the centre of Sydney, we were able to buy this beautiful house and acreage.' She waved her hand to indicate the sprawling backyard. 'Not only do we travel less now, but we also pursue our hobbies at our leisure – Steve's got his beer brewery upfront while we produce honey in our very own hives in the backyard.'

The couple was equally enthralled to hear about our background and our travels and Lou gave us some tips on things to do and see around the Blue Mountains.

As we had just one day, we decided to make the most of the evening, and after freshening up, took a drive into town. Katoomba is a beautiful hilltop village with a small population spread around a decent square block on either side of the Great Western Highway. There is a train line that bisects the town and takes commuters daily to Sydney. The houses that line the main streets are mostly single-storey brick structures built in the early 1900s with beautifully landscaped gardens. The town centre is compact yet charming with busy eateries, heritage resorts, colourful souvenir shops and convenience stores.

Katoomba's southern perimeter borders the stunning Jamieson Valley, home to the iconic Three Sisters rock formation. These three weathered, sandstone peaks formed thousands of years ago through erosion stand proud like sharp projections on the spine of a Jurassic-era dinosaur. In the distance, we could make out the undulating peaks of Ruined Castle and Mount Solitary. The valley was carpeted in a sea of green, and I could appreciate the gentle slope of the plateau from the eastern edge of the Great Dividing Range as it gradually dropped from these towering peaks to near sea level nearer to the coast.

What was hard to appreciate, standing at Echo Point overlooking just one small section of the park, was just how small the valley was in comparison to the Greater Blue Mountains Area – a rugged sandstone tableland covering over 1 million hectares spread across eight adjacent conservation reserves on the eastern periphery of the Great Dividing Range! It is rugged, stunning and vast. Small wonder the early explorers repeatedly failed to find a safe passage through it.

The northernmost part of the protected area is within the Wollemi National Park, roughly 200 kilometres north-west of where we stood. I make special mention of this because it is home to one of the oldest living tree species in the world. Somewhere hidden in the folds of the deep canyons and nestled under the shade of the sheer cliff walls, a group of around one hundred Wollemi pines live and breathe, just as they have done for some thirty million years. The species was thought to have become extinct with the last fossil record dated at about two million years old, however, in 1994 discovery of specimens that were alive and well created a buzz in the botanical fraternity around the world. It was the equivalent of finding a living dinosaur and for that very reason they are called 'Dinosaur Trees'. The dramatic discovery of an evolutionary line thought to be long extinct is even more remarkable when you think they were growing under the very noses of Sydneysiders, a mere 150 kilometres from the most densely populated city in Australia.*

The next morning after a sleep-in we woke to an empty house as Lou and Steve had already left for work. We had a leisurely breakfast on the large back deck and then set out for Evans Lookout where we planned to do one of the many trekking routes that you can take.

The Grand Canyon walk is located in the Blueheath area of the Blue Mountains National Park. The 6.3-kilometre track is well-shaded and meanders through luscious native vegetation of golden wattles, ancient ferns and of course the ubiquitous eucalypts. The sheer cliffs, tumbling waterfalls and ancient rainforests make for an intimate and wholly pleasurable experience. We did the trek in about four hours at a leisurely pace, spending time at Evans Lookout which offers spectacular views of Grose Valley and the near-vertical sandstone cliff walls beyond.

We got back to Lou and Steve's place around 3 p.m., and, after loading up the car and saying a quick goodbye to our hosts, we were on our way to Sydney. I had booked a hostel room in the heart of the city, but we'd decided to break the journey by stopping in the western suburb of Wentworthville, hoping to get into Sydney early the next morning to beat the infamous rush-hour traffic. That at least, was what we had hoped. The reality proved quite different!

Special efforts were made to protect the Wollemi pines when the 2019–20 Australian bushfires burned through the park, a remarkable feat by the local authorities and the brave firemen and conservationists who risked their lives. The NSW fires were especially fierce in this part of the Great Dividing Range and adjacent tablelands. More than 80 per cent of the World Heritage-listed Greater Blue Mountains Area and 54 per cent of the NSW components of the Gondwana Rainforests of the Australia World Heritage zone were affected by the fire.

The 2019–20 bushfires were unprecedented in their extent and intensity. According to one estimate, the catastrophic bushfire season has burned an estimated 10 million hectares, destroyed over 1,400 homes, killed at least 24 people, and killed or displaced an estimated three billion animals.

CHAPTER 24

Emerald City

A good traveller has no fixed plans and is not intent on arriving – Lao Tzu

After leaving Katoomba, we stopped for a night at my relative's unit in Wentworthville. Rey is my mother's first cousin and had migrated to Australia from Dubai a few years ago with his wife Lavina and their two teenage daughters, Jessica and Sarah. I'd had little interaction with either Rey or Lavina before we filed our Australian migration papers; however, they were helpful throughout the process and provided us with a lot of guidance ever since.

Driving around Wentworthville we were surprised with the 'Indian-ness' of the suburb. There were Hindu temples, Indian grocers, and a range of Indian restaurants lining the main street. Ambika even spotted an Indian jewellery store and an Indian beauty parlour. We satiated our craving for Indian food by gorging on hot samosas and jalebis from an Indian grocery store, wolfing them down like two ravenous creatures who hadn't eaten in days. After nearly two months on the road, surviving primarily on Subway sandwiches and crackers, it felt good to taste some Indian delicacies.

The ethnic diversity we saw around us was a reflection of how Australia has evolved over the years. The potpourri of cultures was the result of a succession of economic circumstances, emerging opportunities, political decisions and, at times, sheer ingenuity shown by the country's leaders.

The penal transportation which had started with the first convict landing ended soon after Sydney was incorporated as a city in 1842. The gold rush of the 1850s created a new surge of migrants.

Soon after Australia became a federation in 1901, the federal government passed the *Immigration Restriction Act*, which marked the commencement of the 'White Australia Policy'. During World War II, Prime Minister John Curtin reinforced the policy, saying, 'This country shall remain forever the home of the descendants of those people who came here in peace to establish in the South Seas an outpost of the British race.' I could empathise with this argument, although not necessarily agree with it: the Commonwealth was at the peak of its might across the globe, and British citizens were used to servitude by the coloured people in all the countries in its dominion. Australia was probably the only place where coloured people could work side by side with whites and expect a similar lifestyle as a reward. The colonists had every reason to resent such an arrangement.

Although racism and discrimination against skin colour was a driving force, it was the disparity in working cultures that made coloured people a real threat. Non-whites were used to working long hours, earning low wages and were disinclined to seek compensations from unions. The colonists, on the other hand, after having toiled for over a century, were gradually settling into a comfortable lifestyle. They were unable to accept that such working conditions would go on forever. In fact, Deakin, in his justification of the 'White Australia' policy, remarked: 'It is not the bad qualities, but the good qualities of these alien races that make them so dangerous to us. It is their inexhaustible energy, their power of applying themselves to new tasks, their endurance and low standard of living that make them such competitors.'

Sometime in 1935 the new 'populate or perish' mantra evolved. Immigration Minister Arthur Calwell stated in 1947, 'We have twenty-five years at most to populate this country before the yellow races are down on us.' This led to a new wave of migrants from Europe, mostly Italy, Greece and Yugoslavia.

In March 1966, for the first time, applications were accepted from well-qualified people 'based on their suitability as settlers, their ability to integrate readily and their possession of qualifications positively useful to Australia'. The outcome of this gradual but radical shift in policy was evident in the statistics. By 2010, the post-war immigration program had received more than 6.5 million migrants from every continent. The population tripled in the six decades to around 21 million, comprising people originating from nearly two hundred countries. Australia had emerged as a nation that not only welcomed people from all cultural backgrounds but thrived in the ensuing diversity.

Rey and Lavina lived in a housing complex situated close to the railway station, a strategic decision in a city that struggled with traffic. We sat up till late in the night chatting away – they told us of their initial struggles when they first arrived, and we shared stories of our adventures on the road. Rey ordered in some classic Dum-Biryani for dinner and Ambika and I put up quite a show attacking the food without any cutlery while talking away. Rey and Lavina had a secure and established life in Dubai with a large circle of family and friends. They would have gladly stayed if not for their children and their future prospects in an increasingly interconnected world. Although Dubai was a world-class city in its own right, it did not have many international universities, and sooner or later Rey and Lavina would have been faced with the inevitable decision of sending their girls overseas to study. Australia offered an opportunity to keep the family together, and they jumped at the chance, albeit with a heavy heart to begin with.

Our masterplan to avoid the peak-hour traffic early the next day fell flat even though we left Rey's unit at 5.30 a.m. The bumper to bumper traffic was unbelievable. We averaged only 20 kilometres per hour for the entire drive along the M4 Great Western Highway into Sydney. I was grappling with a range of issues: we had literally arrived from the bush, and I was stressed driving in a large capital city with multi-level crossings, varying speed zones and millions of other vehicles. I was also unfamiliar with the roads and dreaded the fact that I may have to stop and ask for directions. Most of all, I feared I would get on the wrong side of a Sydney-sider who was already running late for an appointment! That would not have been a great start at all.

Eventually, we made it to the Big Hostel on Elizabeth Street, a stone's throw from Central Station and an easy walk to most of Sydney's tourist attractions. In a bid to save a few dollars on parking, we planned to arrive at the hostel before 8 a.m. when most of the inner-city parking lots were free of charge. Due to the slow-moving traffic, we arrived with only a few minutes to spare and played tag team to great effect: park, unload, race to the hostel, Ambika checks in, and I race back to the car and drive away before the stroke of 8 a.m. Parking fines, I had heard, were in the hundreds of dollars, and we had no spare money to give away. The friendly hostel staff on duty managed to bump us up to an en suite room in the far corner of the upper level: a windowless shoebox, slightly bigger than our Melbourne hostel room, but clean and self-sufficient.

Our road trip, which began in Melbourne and took in the Great Ocean Road, the Yarra Valley, Canberra, the Jenolan Caves, Katoomba and ended in an ordinary parking lot in Sydney, lasted nine days and 2000 memorable kilometres. We had driven internationally for the first time in our lives twice during the trip and although it might not seem like such a big deal to most, it definitely was for Ambika and me. We loved every moment of the experience.

When I got back to the hostel after parking the car, Ambika was chatting away with some Greek tourists in the communal kitchen, entirely at home in her new surroundings. Gone was the reserved and cautious girl who entered strangers' homes and budget hostels with scepticism. This trip had converted Ambika into an uber traveller – bold, fearless and willing to take chances. Like the hostel in Melbourne, Sydney's Big Hostel had a universal feel to it with tourists from all around the world mixing freely in the communal areas, speaking in dozens of different languages.

In the afternoon, we stepped out to explore Paddy's Markets near Central Station and the downtown Chinatown area. Lunch was sushi rolls in a small Japanese restaurant tucked away in one of the back alleyways. It was also a time to check our cash reserve and come up with a sightseeing plan for the last few days of our trip. The jingling of coins in Ambika's purse (she was the official accountant) indicated that we were practically broke. Visiting paid tourist sites was thus out of the question. Luckily, Sydney offered plenty of free activities. Within a three-kilometre radius of the iconic Opera House, there were dozens of sightseeing activities on offer. Being the chief planner, I cracked open a Great Northern, opened the city map and pored over it.

At the same time, Ambika practised her skill at using chopsticks, daintily picking up the sushi rolls and adding a dash of wasabi. I neatly divided our options into two categories – excursions which required entry fees, and sights that were free. I crossed out Taronga Zoo ($$$), the Opera House ($$$), the Sydney Eye ($$$), and the Sydney Harbour Bridge Walk ($$$); and instead suggested we ogle the Opera House from the outside, explore the Botanical Gardens on foot, do the much-acclaimed Bondi to Coogee coastal walk, and visit Hyde Park and St Mary's Cathedral. Not a cent would be spent but a lot of ground would be covered. I shared my plan with Ambika and pleased with my ingenuity cracked open another Great Northern to celebrate.

Paddy's Markets and the surrounding Haymarket precinct have a palpable air of business about them. Everywhere we looked, people were moving in a state of constant hurriedness. The vegetable markets and fruit stalls were doing a roaring trade, while street-side cafés, takeaway diners and elegant restaurants were busy handling the afternoon rush hour. Amid the chaos, travellers and backpackers like us wandered about leisurely, window shopping, taking photos of random objects and gawking at the most mundane of things.

Early the next morning, we visited Hyde Park, the oldest park in Australia, a short stroll from our hostel. The expansive, leafy grounds are spread generously across forty acres of prime real estate in the semi-circular shape of a Norman window. Once you enter the park from the southern entrance bordering Liverpool Street, you can, if you so wish, walk in the manicured gardens all the way to Opera House uninterrupted, except for a few arterial roads – a distance of around two kilometres. The parks share common boundaries and a pedestrian would be unaware when a section of the park ends and the other begins, if not for the tourist signs at the entrance gates. Sydneysiders' love for open spaces is evident in the way large tracts of prime land in one of the most expensive and sought after areas have been set aside for public gardens and institutions.

Hyde Park's central avenue of Hill's weeping figs leads to the ANZAC War Memorial and the Pool of Reflection. The park is dotted with lush conifers, palms and a variety of Moreton Bay figs and Port Jackson figs. The ANZAC War Memorial, built to honour the contribution of the Australian Imperial Force during World War I, is an elegant pink granite structure built in traditional Gothic style, and dominates the southern end of the park. The craftsmanship of the construction is eye-catching: characteristic Art Deco buttresses, impressive arched yellow-stained glass windows, and a ziggurat-inspired stepped roof. The exterior is adorned with several bronze friezes, carved granite relief panels and the building is positioned atop a cruciform pedestal.

As we climbed up the broad, imposing steps, we were greeted by a military officer in a striking uniform. We then entered the Hall of Memory, the Memorial's principal commemorative space – an impressive circular room with niches, grand cathedral windows and a tall domed ceiling covered in gold stars. In one corner, a tiny enclave houses the Flame of Remembrance in a flat dish mounted on a pedestal, behind which the flags of Australia, New Zealand and New South Wales stand proud. The centrepiece of the Memorial is the stunning sculpture named *Sacrifice*, intentionally placed in the central Well of Contemplation so that all who enter the Hall must gaze down upon it with reverence and gratitude. The stark sculpture which depicts the weight of the dead young warrior carried on his shield by his mother, sister and wife nursing an infant child encapsulate the message at the heart of the Memorial. The sculptor, George Rayner Hoff, uses the analogy of a Spartan warrior to evoke the emotion experienced by the families of the young men who died in battle.

Outside, we sat by the Pool of Reflection at the northern end, which offers a serene backdrop to the War Memorial. Interestingly, the poplars that flank the pool on both sides are not native to Australia but symbolise the French countryside where Australian soldiers fought and perished.

Hyde Park is filled with many more monuments, sculptures and statues commemorating the achievements of early colonists, but as we were short on time, we were unable to stop and appreciate each and every one of them. We couldn't miss however the magnificent Archibald Fountain sculpture at the northern end of the park. Only a blind person would pass right past without casting at least a sideways glance at this beautiful structure which was commissioned in 1919 by J.F. Archibald, founding editor of the *Bulletin*, to commemorate the association between Australia and France during World War I.

Across the road, the golden-brown sandstone structure of St Mary's Cathedral beckoned us with its imposing twin spires. Also designed in the Gothic style, the history of the cathedral is as old as the history of Sydney and early colonisation itself.

The first settlers in Australia mostly belonged to the Church of England. However, some Irish convicts and settlers were Roman Catholics and did not have anyone to attend to their religious needs. The first Irish priest, Father O'Flynn, travelled to New South Wales but, lacking appropriate government sanction, was sent home. It was not until 1820 that two other priests, Father Conolly and Father John Therry, arrived to officially minister to the Roman Catholics in Australia. Therry claimed that, on the day of his arrival, he had a vision of a mighty church of golden stone dedicated to the Blessed Virgin Mary, its twin spires rising above Sydney's city skyline. The foundation stone for the first chapel was laid in 1821; however, this structure was destroyed by fire in 1865. It took one hundred and eighty long years and three iterations to the building design before the two southern spires were finally installed in 2000 manifesting Therry's grand vision. Today, the cathedral serves as the seat of the Archbishop of Sydney and holds the title and dignity of a minor basilica.

The cathedral is built to impress. The sandstone exteriors are lavish in detail: the flying buttresses of the chancel and nave, the text of the Ave Maria and other invocations carved high up on the walls, the many carved saintly heads which gaze benignly down, the majestic spires. Topped with a red cedar roof, the nave has an open arch-braced construction enlivened by decorative pierced carvings. The floorplan is in the conventional cruciform shape, with a tower over the crossing of the nave and transepts and the twin towers at the south end.

When you enter the church, your eye is drawn forward, along the length of the nave, toward the white pinnacles of the high altar screen, and the vibrant colours of the stained-glass windows which were made in Birmingham, England and depict the coronation of Mary in Heaven with Christ present. The beautiful high altar, as well as the other altars in the chapels, are made from New Zealand Oamaru stone with marble columns and carved alabaster capitals. A relief sculpture of the body of Jesus based on the Shroud of Turin adorns the lower altar. Located beneath the nave, the crypt serves as a sanctuary; the final resting place of some of the most important Catholic leaders in Australia.

After a few minutes of silent prayer, Ambika and I wandered around inside the vast interior. We chanced upon a notice which declared a solemn high mass was due to be celebrated in two days by the cardinal to commemorate the holy sacrament of marriage. Invitations were out for couples reaching significant milestones in their married lives – silver, golden and platinum anniversaries. By pure chance, that day incidentally marked our first wedding anniversary; what were the odds that our presence in this iconic city should coincide with a high mass in one of the most significant cathedrals in Australia? The day would also mark the penultimate day of our grand trip. We could use all the blessings we could get and so we jumped at the chance of attending the mass and enrolled. My business suit and Ambika's formal dress that we'd been lugging around for the entire trip had a definite purpose it seemed, after all.

CHAPTER 25
Showers of Blessings

It is the journey, not the arrival that matters – T.S. Eliot

Our date with God finalised, we continued meandering, entering the sprawling Botanic Gardens via the Crescent Precinct at its southern end. The imposing sandstone structure of the Art Gallery of New South Wales stands proud at the south-eastern edge of the gardens, its grand Ionic pillars supporting an impressive triangular roof and fronting a beautiful façade built from trachyte and freestone. Although Ambika and I were not particularly interested in art galleries, we decided to have a quick look around, especially since the entry was free.

Established in 1871, the gallery is the second oldest in the country (after the National Gallery of Victoria), the leading museum of art in New South Wales and one of Australia's foremost cultural institutions. It holds significant collections of Australian, European and Asian art, as well as an extensive display of local Indigenous art. We wandered around the various galleries appreciating the displayed art, but by the time we got to the contemporary art section, we gave up pretending to understand the finer details! We retraced our steps back to the exit and, not wanting to seem ignorant, unimpressed or worse still disrespectful, collected a bunch of brochures and quietly left, pretending to be in deep discussion.

We wandered down Art Gallery Road towards the harbour and wound up at a point known as Mrs Macquarie's Chair, so named because of an innocuous and uncomfortable looking seat carved out of a sandstone ledge. Situated at the very edge of the shoreline, the seat was specially commissioned by Governor Macquarie in 1810 for his wife Elizabeth who was known to love the area.

We stood at the water's edge and took in the view: the foreshore closest to the semi-circular cove which marked the edge of the Botanic Gardens, the historic Government House which sits on high ground just past the gardens, the gleaming white façade of the iconic Sydney Opera House, and the imposing 'coathanger' shaped Sydney Harbour Bridge with its solid granite pylons. Across Port Jackson, we could see impressive waterfront mansions and apartment blocks dotting the northern shores amid parklands and reserves. The afternoon skies were a deep blue with just a few wisps of cirrus clouds, and the sun shone with splendour on the shimmering waters where hundreds of watercraft raced around: sailing boats, day cruisers, city ferries and recreational vessels.

Sydney Harbour's crowning glory, and with good reason, is the world-famous, snow-white structure of the Opera House. The magnificent building stood proud against the backdrop of the brilliant October sky, its white sail-shaped shells gleaming in the afternoon sun. The beauty of its unconventional design – based on complex sections of a sphere, split into small parts and stacked in random order – was unquestionable. Jørn Utzon, the Danish architect who dreamt up the design, said that it was inspired by the simple act of peeling an orange: the fourteen shells of the building, if combined, would form a perfect sphere. A straightforward concept in principle but, as the engineers working on the project were to discover soon enough, a challenging and cumbersome design to execute. Never before had such a daring concept been brought to life, particularly in a world more familiar with the traditional cube and rectangular designs.

On a personal front, Utzon faced constant criticism and umpteen hurdles from the government and the local community due to the mounting delays and costs. Disgruntled sections of society failed to understand the unique beauty of Utzon's visionary design. In February 1966, Utzon resigned due to the increasing animosity and was unceremoniously dumped from the project. He left Australia soon after, heartbroken, never to return to see his masterpiece completed.

The grand design from concept to completion took sixteen years and cost $102 million – ten years longer and $95 million more than was initially budgeted. The building's official opening was finally commemorated by Queen Elizabeth II on 20 October 1973 amid great fanfare.

Standing at the water's edge of what is arguably one of the most beautiful harbours in the world, you could imagine how the first settlers must have felt when they first sailed in.

The first settlers who arrived in the First Fleet on 18 January 1788 were soon to discover that Botany Bay was not quite the paradise as described by Captain Cook a few years earlier. The bay was open, shallow and unprotected, fresh water was scarce, and the soil was poor. Concerned for the welfare of the people under his charge, Captain Arthur Phillip and an explorer party left on 21 January in three small boats to find a more suitable bay. He sailed north past a beautiful coastline with pristine beaches backed by lush vegetation until he reached what is today known as Watsons Bay, close to the harbour's 'south head'. As he rounded the headland, he beheld Port Jackson and present-day Sydney Harbour. His impressions were recorded in a letter he sent to England later: 'the finest harbour in the world, in which a thousand sail of the line may ride in the most perfect security …'

On 26 January 1788, the entire First Fleet weighed anchor and sailed up the coast to Port Jackson. The site selected for anchorage had deep water close to the shore, was sheltered, and even had a small freshwater stream flowing into it. Phillip named it Sydney Cove, after Lord Sydney, the British Home Secretary at the time. The British flag was officially planted, and possession claimed. Today this date is celebrated as Australia Day, marking the beginning of British settlement history in Australia.

The irony that we chose to end our backpacking journey in the very location where the first white settlers began theirs was not lost on us. The stunning bay views, the iconic location and the rich history of the place held us in its sway, and we could not help but linger around for the entire afternoon. We ambled along the foreshore, around the periphery of the Botanic Gardens, and past the busy Circular quay with its waterfront cafes and local ferries, until we drifted to The Rocks - the birthplace of modern Sydney which retains its heritage charm to date. We enjoyed a sumptuous rooftop lunch at the iconic Glenmore Hotel overlooking the Sydney harbour and later on pampered ourselves even more with some decadent desserts at the Guylian Belgian Chocolate Café. We had a lot to celebrate after all – our first year of marriage, the end of a memorable road trip, and the start of our lives Down Under.

With just a few days to go before we were due to fly back to Brisbane, we decided to do the famous Bondi to Coogee walk – a must-do experience recommended by most travel guides. The clifftop walk extends for six kilometres along the jagged and curvaceous coastline, through one of the most expensive and arguably one of the most sought-after seaside precincts in all of Australia. The walk features stunning cliff views, parks, secluded bays and rock pools. We opted to do the walk in reverse, starting at Coogee. It was another perfect Sydney day, with cloudless blue skies and a light onshore breeze. The ocean was a deep opalescent blue, the distant horizon merging with the skies above. As it was a Saturday, the beaches and parks were filled with people – locals and travellers alike – revelling in the sunshine. The walk offered a perfect introduction to Australia's famed beach culture: daring surfers, watchful lifeguards, beach picnics, community pools, chilled-out cafés, funky locals, secluded coves, community barbecues and picture-perfect beaches.

Beach culture did not happen overnight in Australia, though. The early settlers were not accustomed to sunbathing, picnicking on the beach or even swimming in the ocean wearing bathing costumes – a taboo in those times. It took nearly a century for beach-going to be considered a 'thing'. At first, it was a matter of priorities: the monumental task of nation-building meant the settlers had to concentrate on crossing the Great Dividing Range and finding water, food, farming, timber and mineral wealth. Besides, the ocean was a painful reminder of the arduous voyage they had undertaken and the vast distance that separated them from home.

It wasn't until Australia was federated that people warmed up to the idea of visiting the beach as a leisure activity. The pale-skinned foreigners aligned the beach experience with their British counterparts who picnicked in colder weather. The first beachgoers shunned the very thought of entering the sea, preferring instead to set their picnic basket of cakes, jam tarts and tea on beach mats, a respectable distance from the water. They were also scared of sharks, dangerous sea creatures, deadly rips and undercurrents. Bathing in Sydney Cove and Darling Harbour during daylight hours was banned from 1833; the ban was extended to Sydney's ocean beaches in 1838. Newcastle was one of the first places where the ban was challenged – for a practical reason more than anything else – by mineworkers who wanted to cleanse themselves of the coal dust.

On a warm October morning in 1902, after making his intentions known to the locals, William Gocher waded into the open waters donning a neck-to-knee bathing costume. For this act, the police gave him a minor infringement notice, while his friends gave him a gold watch for his bravado! Beach culture quickly evolved and in November 1903 the reluctant Manly council resolved to allow all-day bathing, provided that neck-to-knee costumes were worn. As cities grew, congestion and pollution created health issues, and doctors began to prescribe sea air and saltwater as tonics for good health. Public transport was becoming more affordable, and the thriving economy meant people had more leisure time. Seaside resorts started popping up around the country and, within a few decades, Australians had well and truly turned into a beach-crazy nation.

The other hurdle in the nineteenth century, however, was a moral one. It is hard to imagine it today, where boardshorts and string bikinis are commonplace, but in the nineteenth century, strict rules were enforced with regards to dress codes and moral conduct while outdoors, especially near the water. The issue was one of modesty as there were no changing sheds and swimming costumes were rare. In fact, for many years, bathing in Australia was segregated by sex. Swimwear that we would recognise as such first appeared in the early twentieth century. Before that, beachgoers waded timidly in the shallow sections of the beaches wearing cumbersome suits made of cotton or wool. Following the shocking appearance of the bikini in the 1950s, swimwear gradually became more revealing, and more importantly, more practical and acceptable.

As we strode along the coastal path, we were able to appreciate all the elements of modern beachside life in Australia. The Coogee to Bondi walk offers visitors a range of options – open parks, children's play areas, beautiful beaches, saltwater baths, enclosed coves and small bays perfect for stand-up paddling and snorkelling. The most impressive of the saltwater baths is the iconic Bondi Icebergs Club at the southern end of Bondi Beach, with its panoramic view of the kilometre-long beach and the entire bay – not to mention an expensive restaurant and café if you're feeling hungry after all that exercise. Dating back to 1929, the original club owes its name to a group of local lifesavers who swam laps of the baths all year round – even during the cooler winter months.

Towards noon and at the end of our coastal walk, we wandered down to the white sands of Bondi Beach – easily the most recognisable in Australia, if not the world, made famous by the hit TV series *Bondi Rescue*, as well as countless movies and TV ads. It is estimated that nearly two million people visit Bondi every year, a mixture of inappropriately overdressed tourists like us and suntanned locals who take every opportunity to flaunt their bodies and their skills with their surfboards and boogie boards. As we dipped our toes in the warm waters, and enjoyed the revelry all around us against the backdrop of a beautiful sunset, on the most iconic beach, and in the most iconic city of Australia, we felt like we had truly arrived.

On Sunday, the penultimate day before our departure, we were due to attend the high mass at St Mary's Cathedral. Ambika, usually a late riser, was up before me and was busy in the communal laundry ironing our formal clothes. 'We are definitely not going in there looking like tramps,' she said.

As we stepped out into the crisp morning, I was certain Sydney's Big Hostel had never seen such well-dressed guests before. The sun was just making an appearance between the high-rise buildings. As we cut across Hyde Park and entered the church, we were astounded at the size of the congregation. Nearly every pew was full of couples dressed to the nines, some old, some young and many with large families in tow. The church was suffused with soft lighting and soul-stirring music sung by the choir. The archbishop and a retinue of priests commenced the celebration with a welcome note. Midway during the mass, the priest invited everyone who'd come to renew their vows to stand up for the blessings. We were one of the dozen-odd couples who formed this part of the congregation. The celebration was as beautiful and meaningful as it was grand and unique. We were given a souvenir photograph, and it remains one of our most prized possessions from the trip.

Our flight back to Brisbane marked our symbolic transition from carefree backpackers in a foreign land to new settlers in a country whose fabric was interwoven with countless other migrant stories. As I drifted in and out of sleep, I re-lived some of the spectacular moments of our journey across this beautiful country. Our shark dive experience at the Sunshine Coast; the spontaneous friendship with Helen and Ann; our *Spirit of Queensland* train ride; the Whitehaven Beach experience; the stunning Millaa Millaa waterfall in the Atherton Tablelands; the magical sunset at Port Douglas; the drive through the ancient rainforests of Cape Tribulation; the unexpected dinner with Frank and his friends in Townsville. I also thought about iconic Melbourne with its moody weather; the spectacular Great Ocean Road drive; the helicopter ride over the Twelve Apostles; the visit to Parliament

House in Canberra; the dark and ancient mysteries of the Jenolan Caves; the renewal of our vows at Sydney's St Mary's Cathedral; and the quiet moments we shared in the Botanic Gardens.

Apart from gaining invaluable insights about Australia and from satiating our unquenching thirst for travel and adventure, these past few months had brought us closer together as a married couple. This trip had accelerated and matured our relationship in a very big way; we had learned a lot about each other – our likes and dislikes, our silly quirks and our admirable traits, things we loved doing together and some things that did not interest the other at all. The journey gave us ample opportunities to get intimate with each other in a way only extended travel can do: to learn about events from our past that shaped us, and our aspirations for the future which motivated us. We were mature enough to not consider this as the ultimate test of our relationship – we knew that life would give us many hard knocks along the way – but, we had trust in our companionship, and knew in our hearts that we had found an ideal partner in each other.

We would have loved to have travelled a little bit further and for a little bit longer. Still to see were the hidden gorges, ancient landscapes and coral bays of the Pilbara; the rainforests of Kakadu; Western Australia's magnificent southern coast and the mysterious Red Centre. All of this would have to wait. We were preparing to shift gears into survival mode as our prospects of employment were still grim, and we weren't sure how many more months we'd be able to manage without an income. Apart from the one job offer while we were in Melbourne, which vanished sooner than it appeared, there was not a single positive lead or any prospective jobs on the horizon. The following few months would be challenging, and with our bank balance dwindling fast, we had no safety net or a fallback plan. If either of us were unsuccessful in securing a job soon we would be compelled to depart Australia, leaving behind the land we had come to love, and say goodbye to all the limitless possibilities it offered – not a comforting thought at all. But we weren't going to go down without a fight. We knew innately that the path would unfold … and just as long as we had each other, things would turn out just fine.

Neither of us regretted our decision to take this trip, though. It was because of this journey that we began to appreciate just how vast, isolated and unique Australia really is. We were also starting to appreciate the core values that shaped the nation – egalitarianism, self-reliance, a fair go, self-deprecation, larrikinism and an acceptance of other cultures. Australians talked more about Australia than anything else, but not in an egotistic way. This country was thousands of miles away from the rest of the world, and this distance was the cause of constant self-reflection. The people here were proud, not rudely or arrogantly so, but rather with a sense of belonging and ownership of the nation's past mistakes, its national ideology and its promising future.

We now had a chance to contribute positively, and we were grateful for this opportunity. As our Boeing 787 touched down at Brisbane Airport, our transformation was complete.

We were ready!

EPILOGUE
Land of the Red Dog

If one advances confidently in the direction of one's dreams, and endeavours to live the life which one has imagined, one will meet with a success unexpected in common hours
– Henry David Thoreau

'This looks and feels like hot wax!' Ambika said as she applied a thin layer of Vegemite to my toast. Made from leftover brewers' yeast, Vegemite was created almost by mistake in 1922 by Cyril Callister in Melbourne. It contains one of the highest sources of B vitamins and can be found in the cupboard of most Australian kitchens. Generations of Australian kids can't imagine growing up without it. It's so famous that pretty much every Australian can hum the Vegemite ad jingle.

The black gooey substance has a peculiar umami taste and like most things uniquely Australian, requires a bit of getting used to. The best way of eating it is on toasted bread with a layer of butter or margarine. However, you only need a tiny amount due to its saltiness and intense flavour. It seemed all right to me, but admittedly I had only recently acquired a taste for it. As Ambika passed me my toast, I deftly extracted the round pit lodged in the fleshy green belly of an avocado, Australia's superfood and part of our staple diet by now. It made for a nice combination along with the Vegemite toast.

We'd parked at one of the rest stops that dot the North West Coastal Highway on our way from Port Hedland to Exmouth. This was our first camping holiday since our daughter Renée was born just a few months earlier. Our four-wheel drive was packed with a tent and camping accessories for what was promising to be a week of discovery and adventure. In the back seat, our toddler son Rohan and baby Renée were blissfully asleep.

The eight-hour drive from Port Hedland to Exmouth takes you through a flat, surreal landscape with miles and miles of pencil-straight asphalt roads and ochre-coloured plains marked by giant termite mounds like freckles on the earth's surface. The Ningaloo region is the gateway to one of the most exotic and pristine destinations in Western Australia – a land where the outback meets the reef. It may not be as popular as some other areas due to its remoteness, but for those who make an effort, the rewards are immense – historic lighthouses, stunning reefs just metres from the coast, chalk-white beaches, azure waters, and even the opportunity to swim with whale sharks, should you be feeling adventurous!

The year was 2019 and it was almost five years since we'd left India. Where had the time gone? One moment we were carefree backpackers and the next we were parents of two beautiful children, on our way to becoming Australian citizens. I'd had three different jobs, and we'd move house five times across two states. There were occasions, particularly during the early days, when I almost gave up and went back to my sailing job. However, we held on to hope and persisted. Our latest move was to the small mining town of Port Hedland – nestled in the remote fringes of the Pilbara region in the North West of Australia and home to the largest bulk export iron ore port in the world. Never in our wildest dreams did we imagine we'd be living in a town of fewer than 15,000 people on Australia's wild north-west Pilbara coast – the land of the iconic, and much loved Red Dog.

As we tucked into breakfast, I reflected on our incredible journey of discovery across three states, thirteen exotic destinations and roughly 5000 kilometres of travel. A minuscule distance in comparison to Australia's eight million square kilometres, but it was a pretty good start. Not only did we have some unforgettable experiences, but we were also afforded an insight into the spirit of this nation and what makes it so unique. Australia is an enigma that can be experienced but never fully understood. That the modern nation even exists is remarkable in itself, let alone the fact that it's thriving and prosperous. I wondered how history might have turned out had Willem Janszoon, the Dutch explorer who reached Australian shores in his boat *Duyfken*, not turned back with a report that the land had no potential for trade, and the natives were unwelcoming. (Janszoon had sailed along the western coast of Cape York and landed near the modern town of Weipa. He continued to map the coastline for another 320 kilometres but incorrectly assumed that it was part of Papua New Guinea.) What might have happened if Captain Cook, like so many other early explorers, had failed to discover the east coast and a suitable landing site at Botany Bay? Or if the *Endeavour* had been destroyed near Cooktown on its way back to England? What if the early colonists were speared to death by the traditional landholders when they first arrived? What if the convicts had mutinied against the authorities? What if the convicts had mutinied against the authorities? What if the early explorers had not found a passage through the Blue Mountains? And what if the gold rush had not happened?

Almost miraculously it would seem, a series of implausible historical events and misadventures led to the birth of a modern nation. Australia forged ahead into the twentieth-century shoulder to shoulder with other developed countries around the world, most of which had existed for far longer.

The first settlers certainly didn't think of Australia as a paradise with unlimited potential. Faced with unknown (and often unrecognisable) dangers, isolated from the rest of the world, and left to their own devices, the colonists – convicts and free settlers alike – had to work hard to tame the land and discover its riches. The harsh continent tested their mettle. Yet time and again they prevailed: through economic recessions, periodic droughts and seasonal floods, intense cyclones and raging bushfires. The most peculiar aspect to us is the fact that the nation's foundation stone was laid by criminals; people banished from Britain to lead a life of exile on distant shores, often for committing the pettiest of crimes.

This island nation has one defining trait above all else – it is a land of contrasts and fresh discoveries.

It's a young nation, but its Indigenous history predates any other living civilisation. It's the world's flattest and driest continent but has regions where rainforests thrive and places where torrential rains and flash flooding are frequent. The country has no predatory animals but is home to some of the most venomous and fearsome creatures on the planet – both on land and in the water. It's a place where convicts became police officers (and this system actually worked!). It's a country ravaged by bushfires and climate extremes, yet it harbours some of the most ancient life forms still in existence. Australia is a country whose citizens defy authority, yet it's one of the safest nations with a mostly law-abiding and peace-loving population. Australia begs to be discovered: who knows what mysteries and wealth lie in its vast interior?

The famous Australian historian Marcus Clarke summed up his country as follows: 'In Australia alone is to be found the Grotesque, the Weird, the strange scribblings of nature learning how to write. Some see beauty in our trees without shade, our flowers without perfume, our birds who cannot fly, and our beasts who have not yet learned to walk on all fours. But the dweller in the wilderness acknowledges the subtle charm of this fantastic land of monstrosities. He becomes familiar with the beauty of loneliness … the phantasmagoria of that wild dreamland called the Bush interprets itself, and he begins to understand why free Esau loved his heritage of desert sand better than all the bountiful richness of Egypt.' These few lines capture the true essence of Australia and its people.

Our first five years in Australia have led us to believe it's an egalitarian country that accepts cultures and races from around the world without prejudice. While the rest of the world moves on at a break-neck speed, Australia prefers to advance in slow, measured steps. Most of the Australians we met – and most of the historical figures referenced in this book –

showed some unique defining traits: stoic resilience, a dry sense of humour and a healthy dash of homegrown humility.

Money is essential to living a good life in Australia, but money does not necessarily create a divide between the rich and the poor. It is a land of the underdog after all and Australians frown upon vulgar and extravagant displays of wealth. The real wealth of the nation is not measured in its material richness but in the richness of spirit, an admirable trait that shines through in the darkest of days.

Our journey as new migrants has been a rewarding and enriching experience. And what a journey it has been! We have assimilated into Australian society, made many friends - some neighbours, some work colleagues and some chance encounters. With two young children, our lives have taken on a new meaning and we now look forward to exploring the world through their eyes.

As I put away the camping table and dishes after breakfast that morning, Ambika, who was leafing through a second-hand road atlas, chanced upon a full-page ad enticing readers to sample the rugged beauty of New Zealand, Australia's Tasman cousin. She casually remarked, 'This place looks so heavenly. I wonder what it'd be like to go on a campervan trip with our kids someday?'

I'm holding onto this dream ... You never know, it may just come true.

BIBLIOGRAPHY

CHAPTER 2 – Lift Off
https://theconversation.com/longing-for-the-golden-age-of-air-travel-be-careful-what-you-wish-for-34177
2016 AACTA Awards Paul Hogan Tribute: https://www.youtube.com/watch?v=b1emKdyZjYI

CHAPTER 4 – A River Runs Through It
https://www.nla.gov.au/unbound/lost-shipwrecked-saved
https://www.amw.org.au/content/convict-records-queensland-1825-1842

CHAPTER 5 – Of Strange Beasts and Distant Lands
https://www.australiangeographic.com.au/topics/science-environment/2012/07/australias-10-most-dangerous-snakes/

CHAPTER 6 – Heads we go North!
https://www.exodus2013.co.uk/the-ten-pound-pom /
http://www.pandosnco.co.uk/ten_pound_poms.html

CHAPTER 8 – Romancing the Railways
https://www.telegraph.co.uk/travel/destinations/oceania/australia/articles/The-Ghan-Great-Train-Journeys/
https://www.telegraph.co.uk/travel/destinations/oceania/australia/articles/australia-indian-pacific-railway/

BIBLIOGRAPHY

https://www.humanrights.gov.au/our-work/race-discrimination/publications/australian-south-sea-islanders-century-race
https://www.abc.net.au/news/2017-12-09/tracks-robyn-davidson-remembers-epic-desert-trek-40-years-on/9239780
https://www.sbs.com.au/language/english/punjabi-pioneers-revolutionize-blueberry-farming-in-australia

CHAPTER 9 – Heart of the Reef
http://www.greatbarrierreef.org/about-the-reef
http://www.gbrmpa.gov.au/the-reef/reef-facts

CHAPTER 11 – Ancient Land and Old Culture
https://www.aboriginalheritage.org/history/history/
https://www.history.com/news/dna-study-finds-aboriginal-australians-worlds-oldest-civilization

CHAPTER 12 – Inside a Picture Postcard
http://www.tropicalnorthqueensland.org.au/articles/top-waterfalls-atherton-tablelands/
https://www.athertontablelands.com.au/

CHAPTER 13 – Where the Rainforest meets the Reef
https://queenslandhistory.org/2019/08/from-the-archives-possession-island/
https://www.destinationdaintree.com/locations/the-bloomfield-track
https://australianstogether.org.au/discover/australian-history/1967-referendum/
https://australianstogether.org.au/discover/australian-history/stolen-generations
https://www.smithsonianmag.com/smart-news/dna-tests-suggest-aboriginal-australians-have-oldest-society-planet-180960569/

CHAPTER 14 – Shipwrecked
   https://www.nla.gov.au/events/cooks-treasures/papers/Iain-Mc-Calman-Turtlepower-NLACook.pdf
   https://www.nma.gov.au/explore/features/european_voyages/european_voyages_to_the_australian_continent/empire/endeavour_runs_aground
   http://southseas.nla.gov.au/journals/cook/17700817.html
   https://www.sl.nsw.gov.au/learning/captain-james-cook

CHAPTER 15 – Daal, Roti and War Stories
   https://apps.des.qld.gov.au/heritage-register/detail/?id=601129
   https://www.abc.net.au/news/2015-04-22/indias-forgotten-soldiers-who-fought-alongside-anzacs/6406086
   https://www.awm.gov.au/collection/E84294
   https://www.awm.gov.au/articles/atwar/first-world-war
   https://www.awm.gov.au/articles/second-world-war
   https://www.theguardian.com/world/2018/oct/27/armistice-centenary-indian-troops-testimony-sacrifice-british-library
   https://www.awm.gov.au/commemoration/anzac-day/traditions
   http://www.diggerhistory.info/pages-battles/ww2/darwin.htm
   https://nzhistory.govt.nz/war/the-gallipoli-campaign/landing-plans
   https://india.embassy.gov.au/ndli/pa2315.html
   https://www.historylearningsite.co.uk/world-war-one/india-and-world-war-one/

CHAPTER 17 – The Gold Rush
   https://www.oldtreasurybuilding.org.au/past-exhibitions/gold-rush/

CHAPTER 18 – The Grand Dame
   https://www.historychannel.com.au/articles/race-stops-nation-melbourne-cup/

BIBLIOGRAPHY

CHAPTER 19 – Twelve Apostles
https://vicflora.rbg.vic.gov.au/flora/bioregions/otway-range
https://www.lightstation.com/explore-cape-otway/lighthouse/
https://greatoceanroadmelbournetours.com.au/attractions/shipwreck-coast/
http://www.visit12apostles.com.au/port-campbell-visitor

CHAPTER 21 – Seat of Power
https://www.nca.gov.au/siting-and-naming-canberra
https://www.aph.gov.au/Visit_Parliament/Things_to_Do/Discover_the_architecture
https://www.nca.gov.au/factsheet/building-canberra-1958-0
https://www.aph.gov.au/About_Parliament/House_of_Representatives/Powers_practice_and_procedure/00_-_Infosheets/Infosheet_2_-_A_typical_sitting_day

CHAPTER 22 – Dark Caves and New Discoveries
https://www.nma.gov.au/defining-moments/resources/blue-mountains
https://www.jenolancaves.org.au/about/history-of-jenolan-caves/royal-visit-1927/

CHAPTER 23 – Into the Blue
https://www.bluemts.com.au/info/about/history/history-detail/
https://www.environment.nsw.gov.au/topics/parks-reserves-and-protected-areas/fire/park-recovery-and-rehabilitation/recovering-from-2019-20-fires/understanding-the-impact-of-the-2019-20-fires
https://www.rbgsyd.nsw.gov.au/Science/Our-work-discoveries/Germplasm-Conservation-Horticulture/Wollemi-Pine-Conservation-Program/Wollemi-Pine-FAQs/Why-was-it-so-extraordinary
https://www.bbc.com/news/world-australia-50951043
https://www.climatesignals.org/events/australia-bushfire-season-2019-2020

CHAPTER 24 – Emerald City
    https://www.nma.gov.au/defining-moments/resources/postwar-immigration-drive
    https://www.nma.gov.au/defining-moments/resources/end-of-white-australia-policy
    https://www.sydneyoperahouse.com/our-story.html

CHAPTER 25 – Showers of Blessings
    https://www.stmaryscathedral.org.au/

EPILOGUE – Land of the Red Dog
    https://www.nationalgeographic.com.au/history/australias-first-cops-were-all-criminals.aspx
    https://australianhistory.org/willem-janszoon/

ACKNOWLEDGEMENTS

First and foremost, a big thanks to all the people whom we met along the way and who helped us with our transition into Australia as migrants. Our settlement journey would have been quite bumpy and long if not for their advice and support. Most of them barely knew us to begin with, yet they welcomed us without reservations. Heartfelt thanks also for agreeing to allow me to include their stories in this book.

An essential part of our experience also has been our interaction with local Australians, and I would like to thank all our Airbnb hosts who made the trip especially memorable and likewise for allowing me to share their stories.

I am indebted to all the people who helped me get this book published – I wish to express my profound thanks to Rod Morrison for his editorial input – thanks to his amazing skills, the content of this book was transformed from the random musings of a wandering mind into a story anybody could read with particular interest, and hopefully, really enjoy.

Further, thanks to Pauline O'Carolan for proofreading the book and pointing out all the not-so-glaring errors and omissions.

A special note of thanks to Simon Evans for his critique and feedback as a reader.

I would like to thank Daintree Marketing Co-operative Ltd. for allowing me to include some of their content regarding 4WD adventures in Chapter 11. I am also grateful to Kemp James, veteran and former infantryman, for providing insight into Australia's war history.

And last but not least, I am grateful to my family, close friends and associates, whom I troubled no end to proofread the book or to provide feedback while the manuscript and book cover was being finalised.

Thank you for purchasing 'Red Earth Diaries'.

I know you could have picked any number of books to read, but you picked this book and for that, I am extremely grateful.

I hope that you enjoyed reading the book. If so, it would be nice if you could recommend the book on social media - Facebook, Twitter and Instagram.

I hope that you could also take some time to post a review on <u>Goodreads</u> *as well as on* <u>Amazon</u> *or the online bookstore where you purchased this book.*

Simply search for the book title 'Red Earth Diaries' and choose the 'Write a Review' option.

I want you to know that your review is very important to me, and I thank you for taking the effort to provide your feedback.

I appreciate your time and look forward to hearing from you!

Jason Rebello
www.evolvingwordsmith.com
www.theevolvingbackpacker.com